DATE DUE

	PRINTED IN U.S.A.

BARRON'S

The
AFFLUENT
INVESTOR

Financial Advice to Grow and Protect Your Wealth

Phil DeMuth, Ph.D.

Introduction by Ben Stein

All inquiries should be addressed to:
Barron's Educational Series, Inc.
250 Wireless Boulevard
Hauppauge, NY 11788
www.barronseduc.com

ISBN: 978-0-7641-6564-1

Library of Congress Cataloging-in-Publication Data

DeMuth, Phil, 1950-
   The affluent investor : Financial Advice to Grow and Protect Your Wealth / by Phil DeMuth.
      pages cm
   Includes bibliographical references and index.
   ISBN 978-0-7641-6564-1 (alk. paper)
   1. Rich people--Finance, Personal. 2. Investments. I. Title.
   HG179.D42 2013
   332.6--dc23
                              2012048700

PRINTED IN THE UNITED STATES OF AMERICA
9 8 7 6 5 4 3 2 1

Contents

Introduction by Ben Stein

Let's start with a few simple propositions:

1. It is good to have money. Life is happier, more peaceful, and at the same time more exciting if you have money. If you have enough to be considered "affluent," that's even better.

2. It is good to make money with the money you have. Once you have a decent amount of money, it is a marvelous sight to see it growing into more money. To see money growing without you having to work and slave over a hot oven is glorious.

3. Generally speaking, it takes a certain amount of knowledge about money and investing to make your money grow at a satisfactory rate. Money can be lost, can disappear, and can grow negatively, so to speak, if it is handled without knowledge of how investments and money and taxes and law work. In investing, ignorance is not bliss; it's disaster.

4. It is extremely good to have friends who know a lot about money and will share that knowledge with you in extreme detail for free or almost free.

Now, meet Phil DeMuth. Phil is your new fellow passenger on the cruise ship called Life as you pass in the wink of an eye from eternity to eternity, as a poet said in slightly different words. Phil is an amazingly smart guy who has the amazing gift of a spectacular, one in a million work ethic that has made him into a genuine scholar of investing cautiously, carefully–oh, so very carefully–and successfully.

Phil is a very tall, very brilliant guy who has made the study of how investments behave his life's work, aside from caring for his beloved family. For a lucky few well-heeled investors, Phil handles some or all of their fortunes with gimlet-eyed care. He does nothing risky or dangerous, and he is not a gunslinger. He cannot defeat the market or real world circumstances.

But within the context of the real and the actual, Phil does brilliant work. I am not going to give a testimonial to his actual results because I am a client of his and clients are not allowed to give testimonials as to results. That's the law.

Let me just say I would be very sad if he retired.

But now, with the ownership and reading of this book, Phil is going to work for you. (Yes, you have to read it. It is not enough to just buy it.)

I met Phil because I had been friends with his wonderful brother, Chris, for many years because Chris had worked with my father at The American Enterprise Institute. When I first met Phil, he was a psychologist with a love of writing—and with an extreme interest in investing. He had come from Cleveland to Los Angeles with a view to becoming a writer, but also with a compulsion to invest money intelligently.

It was I, yes, little me, who had years of talks with Phil about the markets and about psychology and about writing in Hollywood and finally was able to tell him the truth about himself. He loved psychology. He loved writing. But above all, he was compelled, fascinated, by the behavior of investments and markets.

He was as fascinated by the behavior of different kinds of investment vehicles as a kid in the 1950's might have been about the batting averages of Mickey Mantle and Roger Maris and the earned run average of Whitey Ford. He loved to read about investments, run simulations on his computer, and tell me and anyone else who would listen what he had learned.

I may say that at a certain early stage in Phil's life, I started him on some investment theorems: that you almost never beat the indexes (preached to us by the greatest friend the small investor ever had, John Bogle) and the only way to even reasonably try is with Berkshire-Hathaway; that it's nonsense to say that you cannot time the market–you can't time it day by day or week by week, but when you buy when P/E's are low and Price/Dividend is low, and just plain ratio of price vs. long term average of price is low, you will make a lot more money over the decades than if you buy when those metrics are high. Otherwise price itself would have no meaning, as we often said to ourselves.

Phil and I started writing books about investing with the theorem about timing the markets as our first essay into the world of authorship as co-authors. We established a close working relationship based on a simple principle: Phil would do all of the work and I would take half of the credit and royalties.

It worked well and Phil and I had several Amazon and *New York Times* best sellers....with Phil doing ever more sophisticated analysis and conclusions and me along for the ride.

Now, I have to say ruefully, Phil is off on his maiden solo voyage and he is now your shipmate and colleague, fellow investors. And what a ride you will have. For the price of this book—which is basically free in today's world—you will get the benefit of Phil's years of scholarship, experience, and insight into how to make your money—assuming you start with a meaningful amount—grow into a much more meaningful amount.

It is an almost unbelievable bargain: you get one of the brainiest guys out there, who has studied carefully the works of the other smartest guys out there, telling you how the smart guys make money with relative safety (there is no complete safety ever and no complete success ever), with sanity, with prudence, and with the wind of experience and trial and error at your back—and for this you pay about what it costs to buy a few gallons of gasoline.

In other words, it is basically free—Phil has basically done all of this work for you for free.

I absolutely do not promise that reading this book will make you rich. Phil absolutely does not promise that either. But what I do say is that Phil has seen what has worked in the past and what will therefore almost surely work in the future unless Zombies take over the world. ("What is past is prologue," as it says upon a pedestal at The National Archives.) He offers it up to you on a silver platter of wit and wisdom. Based upon my experience and my knowledge of Phil, unless your uncle is Warren Buffett and he put you in Berkshire-Hathaway when you were 10, in 1967, and kept it there, you cannot find a kinder, more thoughtful investment thinker than Phil.

The time to start in with him on your shoulder is right now. You are making a serious mistake if you delay any longer than you already have. After all, what better use of your time do you have today than learning how to make your family safer, more secure, and richer? Anyone know? Anyone, anyone?

Chapter One: Are You Affluent?

"Let me tell you about the very rich. They are different from you and me."

—F. Scott Fitzgerald, *"The Rich Boy"*

Having written seven investing books for the general public with my pal, economist Ben Stein*, I wanted to write something more narrowly addressing the needs of people like my clients, the high-net-worth investors. I have knocked around the financial services business for a while now and picked up a few crumbs of local knowledge to pass along. There are lots of investment books for beginners, but the affluent investor is actually an underserved market segment. Most of what is dished up for them is just marketing mumbo jumbo designed to ensnare them in Wall Street's wealth expropriation machine.

Let's start by tossing out some numbers. When it comes to our rank in the social beehive, all kinds of people want to find out how much money we have. They don't synchronize watches when collecting data, which means that some data sets are more recent than others, and they measure different parameters. Some track household income. Some track personal income. Some track family income. Wealth is also about savings. Some surveys classify people according to their investable assets. Because they are all based on

---

* When I refer in the text to "Ben," I invariably mean Ben Stein, as opposed to, say, Ben-Hur.

samples that contain sampling error, there is no guarantee that their findings will agree. The figures below are from the Federal Reserve's Survey of Consumer Finances, the Census Bureau, and the World Top Incomes Database, among other places. You will not be able to speed-read through them. I suggest that you pause and reflect upon each figure before going on to the next.

- If you have a net worth (assets minus liabilities) of $4.2 billion, congratulations! You have a net worth equal to the average of the top 400 wealthiest Americans, according to *Forbes Magazine*. The good news here is that it only takes $1.1 billion to crash this party.

- In 2009, the 400 highest taxpayers in the nation (the "Fortunate 400") had an average adjusted gross household income of $202,400,000 apiece. Sadly, this was down 25 percent from 2008, when it was $271,500,000.

- In 2010, to break into the top 1/100th percent of household incomes (including capital gains), you had to earn at least $7,890,307 that year.

These people are rich. They are different from you and me. This is not a book for people like Nathan Pelz, worth $970 million, who said, "You see these guys worth $3 to $4 billion, and you think to yourself, 'What have I done wrong?'" To get to those of us who are affluent rather than rich, we have to step down by an order of magnitude.

- In 2009, there were just over one million households with a net worth (not counting their primary residence) of $5,000,000.

■ In 2010, the top one-tenth of one percent of households had incomes of $1,492,175. That is about 146,000 households— enough to populate a city the size of Austin, Texas (they don't all live in Austin, though).

■ In 2010, the number of U.S. households with a net worth of $1,000,000 or more (not counting their primary residences) was 8.4 million—about 7 percent of the total.

■ That same year, about 30 million households—25 percent of the total—had investable assets of over $100,000.

■ The top 10 percent of U.S. families in 2010 had an average income of $347,754.

Those numbers are skewed, because a disproportionate amount of the average comes from the richest people pulling it up at the top. Let's cut this down to size.

■ To crash into the top 10 percent in 2010, your family had to have an income of over $107,024. To be in the top 5 percent, your family had to have an income of over $150,400. To make it into the top 1 percent, your income had to be over $352,055.

■ But wait—there's more! To be listed in the top ½ of 1 percent, your threshold family income was $521,246 in 2010. Top 1/10th of 1 percent: more than $1,492,175.

■ To be in the top 10 percent of U.S. families by net worth in 2010, your family had to have a net worth of over $952,500. The average net worth within that group was $3,681,880.

■ Looking at individual salaries, the top 1 percent of workers earned $250,000 or more.

■ However, where you live also makes a difference. To make it into the top 1 percent in Stamford, CT, you need a household income of $908,000. But if you move to Jamestown, PA, you'll only need $176,000.

■ The top 5 percent of individual workers would have earned at least $100,000.

■ An upper-middle-class person, with earnings in the top decile that year would have started at $77,500.

■ The median income of a male over age 25 who worked full time was $48,202 in 2011.

It's a relative world. Compared to the average wage earner in the U.S., someone making $250,000 a year is rich. But compared to the really rich among us, the person making $250,000 is a flea.

■ According to economic historian Angus Maddison, the world's gross domestic product averaged $467 per person in year 1 of our era.

■ By 1820 this only had grown to $666 per year.

…Which means that, compared to all people who have ever lived, the worker earning the median $48,202 a year is Bill Gates. Almost everyone who has ever lived has lived in extreme poverty by our standards. We inhabit a world of luxury and opportunity unimaginable to our forefathers, to whom we would appear as a race of supermen living in a land of dreams. Any king who lived before the nineteenth century would faint if you dropped him off at Costco.

While it is perennially fashionable to guillotine the 1 percent, this is an intelligent and hard-working group who make enormous contributions to our society (including paying 28 percent of the total federal income tax and 30 percent of all philanthropy). Unfortunately, the rich have done a bad job defusing class envy. While the rich are the ostensive targets, those who are merely affluent—the so-called millionaires, billionaires, and gazillionaire's earning $250,000 a year—are the real casualties. You can take a lot of money from rich people and they will still be rich. When you tax the affluent at high rates, you stop them in their tracks. They spin their wheels faster but cannot get ahead.

The current income distribution is not a static picture. There is a great deal of income mobility in our society. It is not like ancient Babylonia where the station you were born into was where you stayed for life. White collar workers are comparatively poor early in their careers, but their earnings ramp up rapidly. At the other end of the spectrum, it surely does not go unnoticed among the Forbes 400 that a couple of dozen from their rank roll off the scroll every year, and we're not just talking about those who have gone on to the Happy Hunting Ground. In a competitive society, there are always people eager to climb over your back to get to the top of the greasy pole, and many people are only rich for a while before sliding down. According to JP Morgan, only 15 percent of the Forbes 400 stayed on the list over a 21-year period. Fully one-third of the highest quintile of earners in 2001 had moved out by 2007, and one-third of the top 1 percent of earners in 2007 were not in the top 1 percent of earners in 2009.

The affluent investor can be broadly defined as a person or family who has between $100,000 and $10,000,000 in investable financial assets. This ignores income from labor, from private businesses, and the value of personal residences, all of which might be large or small, but are not our focus here. This is primarily a book about investing. It is not particularly a book for people with $100,000,000 to invest, although they are getting fleeced like everyone else and could learn a lot from it. When Silicon Valley CEOs are flown to New York on private jets to meet with presidents of major banks and given a 1 percent mortgage loan as a sign-on bagatelle, far from having entered a higher plane of banking, they are just rubes with extra zeroes in their checking accounts. If I could choose to be made heir to one of two original $100,000,000 family fortunes, and family "A" has invested in three index funds at Vanguard for the past thirty years, while family "B" has relied on the ministrations of Dodson and his devoted team at the family office in Beacon Hill over the same period, I would choose Family "A" in a blink.

We can further divide affluent investors into two groups: those with $100,000 to $999,999, who are the mass affluent, and those with $1,000,000 to $10,000,000, who are the high net worth. This is roughly how those terms are used in the financial services industry, although the cutoffs vary.

This definition is crude. If you are a retired 62-year-old couple with $100,000 in total savings, you are far from affluent. If you are a 22-year-old hedge fund buckaroo who jingles when he walks, you may only have $100,000 in the bank, but you are already rich.

An infamous internal memo at Merrill Lynch once described those with less than $100,000 in assets as "poor" people. There is something contemptible about classifying people this way. I don't know why, but people who work around large sums of money all day seem to lose their humility and humanity. For a young person to save $100 is a miracle, given all the competing uses for his marginal dollar. For $100 in savings to grow to $200 is a staggering achievement. On the other hand, for someone with $10,000,000 to turn it into $15,000,000 does not seem particularly impressive; it seems like a foregone conclusion (or at least, it used to...).

The affluent and the high net worth are usually the same people at two different points in their lives, younger and older. While I will be talking mostly to the high net worth, my hope is that the affluent will be able to set things up correctly earlier on in their lives so that they can become high net worth sooner. Procrastination is expensive. Life is inevitably full of potholes, but when it comes to your finances, it is a minefield.

MR. & MS. AFFLUENT

Beyond these statistics, if you fall into the affluent category, I can hazard a few educated guesses about you.

You are at least in your forties, and probably part of a two-earner household. It took you time to accumulate this nest egg, and young people typically do not earn or save enough to amass wealth. If you are high net worth, you are blowing out fifty-plus candles on your birthday cake.

You are married, once or twice, and have no more than three children, because they are so fabulously expensive and time-consuming. Children are nature's antidote to inequality, causing even great wealth to regress to the mean eventually.

You are well-educated, possibly with an advanced or professional degree from a highly-regarded school. So is your partner, since well-educated people marry each other. There is no mystery here: educational attainment correlates directly to higher career achievement. You are high-IQ types, and this has fueled your rise up the corporate letterhead. Yes, you are the smartest person in the room (but then you already knew that). You were raised in a family that stressed education and hard work as keys to getting ahead.

You are a small business owner. The top 10 percent of families have 25 percent of their net worth in privately held enterprises. When I visited Ben's country club in Rancho Mirage, I was struck by how many members were small business owners from the Midwest who had sold their firms and retired to palmier climes near the 18th hole. Another choice for your occupation would be: corporate executive. Possibly you are a doctor or lawyer or other highly-paid professional. You also could be an heir or widow to any of the above.

At work, you perform a specialized, technical task. As Adam Smith noted in *The Wealth of Nations*, the prosperity of an economy is closely linked to how differentiated it is. In a tribe in New Guinea, there is not much productivity and not much specialization. Some people hunt, some people gather, some people raise children, and that's about it as far as job descriptions go. The chief may have a few more trinkets than the others, but one person is about as well-off as the next, and there isn't much wealth to go around anyway. In a complex economy, high income workers perform difficult, essential tasks and are paid a premium. This is why your long education (at school or on-the-job) was necessary.

It follows, then, that you work in a major metropolitan area and probably live in one of the better suburbs ringing it. Urban areas are where work is the most differentiated, and therefore where remuneration is the highest (if also where it costs the most to live). The more urban, the more specialized, and the more prosperous.

I have a few guesses about your psychological makeup as well.

THE GREAT DEPRESSION

You are from the last generation to grow up in the shadow of the Great Depression. The difference between people with this background and those who came later is night and day. Pop culture has erased the Great Depression from our collective memory, relegating it to the status of Roman history or World War II: something that might have happened but is of little relevance to cool kids today.

This is not to say you experienced the Great Depression directly, but your parents or grandparents did, and its effect on them made an indelible imprint on you. You might say that the Great Depression became part of your transgenerational family superego. An observation from Samuel Butler's *The Way of All Flesh* (1903) describes this kind of outlook in chilling terms:

> *Most men, indeed, go coolly enough even to be hanged, but the strongest quail before financial ruin....Loss of money indeed is not only the worst pain in itself, but it is the parent of all others.*

The Great Depression was a school that taught that no matter how much you have, it can all be taken away. It can be taken away by a severe downturn in the economy. It can be taken away by fraud and bad investments. It can be taken away by the government. The government can take your money or valuables directly, by confiscation and taxation, or indirectly, by inflation or war. There is no shortage of examples.

As a result, your biggest concern is hanging on to what you've got. It is far more important to you that you not lose a lot of money than it is for you to make a lot more money. In other words, you have become conservative. In spite of being affluent, you are afraid of running out of money.

Because the Great Depression was a time of 25 percent unemployment, you are keenly aware of the value of work. In the 1930s, when most Americans had a high school diploma at best, one of the salient lessons was the importance of getting an education and then finding and keeping a job. People also acquired the ability to get along with others and to work cooperatively. These skills were honed both in the armed services and on the home front during the exigencies of World War II. They accepted the fact that the world did not revolve around them; that it was their duty to fit in and help pull the train forward.

This attitude has served you well financially, although the time you devote to work may have taken its toll in other spheres of your life. Nothing is free. At a recent business dinner, I noticed that everyone at our table was a workaholic. I rhetorically asked, what had happened to the idea of a balanced life—work, family, friends, hobbies, vacations, and so on? One of them replied, "You mean, like Europeans?" and everyone laughed.

Alas, money has not made you happy. At an income over $60,000, more money evidently does not buy much more happiness. Happiness always recedes like a mirage somewhere financially ahead of where you are today. Earned money makes people much happier than free money, which explains why lottery winners are such a miserable lot and so many wealthy heirs struggle with self-worth.

You are concerned that your children have failed to assimilate these values. Relative to how you grew up, they are spoiled. They have expensive educations, but it is an open question how much good it has done them.

WEALTH

I overheard two young actresses talking at the Urth Café in West Hollywood. One of them was explaining to the other how she was glad she wasn't a millionaire. If she had a million dollars, she would have to worry about mansions and cars and servants and all of that. This is how the world looks to someone making $15,000 a year. Life has changed since the screwball comedies of the 1930s, with their Daddy Warbucks patriarchs and madcap heiresses. Regrettably, a million dollars no longer plants you in an estate with a grouse moor. You're not collecting Fabergé eggs.

Even if you have $5,000,000 in the bank, you don't feel rich. I have a friend whose father earned $400 a week. After years of hard work and 18 hour days that routinely included sleeping at the office, he held a check in his hand for $5,000,000. I asked him how he felt. "Deeply humbled," he replied. In other words, you don't feel like a top hat-wearing millionaire. You feel middle-class. A recent study by Fidelity indicates that the typical millionaire with $3.5 million in investable assets feels he would need $7.5 million to be wealthy. Rich people seem to worry about money as much as anyone else. The only man who feels rich is the man who loves what he has.

Your primary financial concern is providing for retirement. You wonder if you have saved enough. Your fallback plan is to work until you're 80, 80 being the new 65. You want to make sure your family is provided for. If there's money left over, you want it to be used wisely, probably for charity.

The fact that you have money does not make you are an ace investor. Like everyone else, you are overconfident in your abilities here. You think because you are good at whatever you do for a living, it should follow that this makes you a snappy investor. This is demonstrably false. You trade too much. You buy high and sell low, letting your emotions sabotage you. You invest on tips and hunches. You approach investing with a gambler's mentality of wins and losses. You don't have a 30,000-foot view of your holdings, and you don't have a rational allocation among them or any set discipline that you follow. Essentially, you do it by the seat of your pants. If someone ran your investments for you the way you run them for yourself, you would fire him. If you already have "helpers," you secretly wonder if they're doing you any good or—worse—if they are just after your money.

THE PLAN

We're going to start by surveying what has brought you to this point, and what you need to do to stay on course and move to the next square on the game board.

Next, we are going to talk about how you invest, and the factors that are important in tailoring your portfolio to your individual profile, including what you do, how much you have, and your life-stage.

Then we're going to roll up our sleeves and go into the port-folio specifics. We're going to review the state of our financial knowledge and, armed with what we know about your personal situation, bring your investing up to the 1960s by buying you the Market Portfolio. Surprisingly, many people you know are still investing the way people did before Alaska became a state. If you want to do more, we have plenty of ideas on that in our bag of tricks. We will talk about investing during retirement and how to draw down your nest egg so that you squeeze the most from it.

Finally, we will go into some financial planning issues filed under the heading of "Asset Protection." We're going to talk about insurance, taxes, estate planning, and the like. I'll bet you find something there that will justify the price of this book many times over. In other words, we will talk about hanging on to what you've got. Which, come to think of it, would be a good subtitle for the book as a whole.

Chapter Two: Rules for Riches

Most people who buy travel magazines do not winter in St. Biarritz. Most people who buy diet books do not become thin.

In a similar vein, the genre known as "GRQ" (Get Rich Quick) literature will surely have many disenchanted readers. You can't get rich quick. You only get rich slowly, over a lifetime of effort. Fantasizing about being rich does not take you there.

Unless you are an heir or you married someone well-heeled—and, as Kip Hubbard observed, no one works harder for his money than the person who marries it—your life has been largely about transforming your human capital into financial capital. This is slow cooking.

Your human capital is the value of your labor, augmented by your education and work habits and anything else that can translate into value in the marketplace. For instance, you might look like a runway model. Or, perhaps you can shoot hoops well enough to compete in the NBA. People like these are exceeding few and their ranks generally do not include you or me. Even in less than industrial-strength doses, though, personal qualities make a big contribution. Being charismatic will help open doors in almost any enterprise.

If you have an outgoing, friendly personality, you will naturally fit in better than someone who is prickly. If you are flexible and willing to relocate and travel, you are far more widely employable than an immoveable object. If you have a big social network, you have more opportunities than someone who sits home alone watching TV. If you play golf or tennis, you will have more valence bonds available to connect with the high-ranking animals. All these constitute an important part of your human capital, although they are seldom the main course.

GET SMART

Education is still the yellow brick road, even if Oz isn't what it used to be. One hundred years ago, there were lots of intelligent Americans who lacked formal schooling. If women worked at all outside the home, they were secretaries, nurses, or teachers. Jews were tailors. Blacks were field hands or porters or similar low-wage earners. Opportunities to move up were limited by the de facto caste system. This is no longer true: with government loans for all, nearly anyone can get a college degree. The long-term value of attending any private college outside the top dozen or so schools on Forbes Top Colleges list is open to question if you have to pay the full tariff. The midlist schools are about to be made irrelevant by competency-based online education. Even an Ivy League diploma seems to be a wasting asset. Ben's daughter-in-law recently went looking for a nanny to take care of her baby while she went back to school. Ben asked her if she found anyone good in the stack of applicants. "Oh yes," she replied, "several of them went to Harvard."

With degree inflation and a superabundance of supply, the advantage of a college education has flattened. Even professional credentials are not the golden tickets they once were: just ask your doctor what he thinks about the practice of medicine these days or your lawyer what he thinks about the practice of law. However, there is no reliable alternative. The graduate degree has become the new BA. Getting as much specialized education as inexpensively as you can in an area where there is a lively labor market is going to be your best plan, even if it does not repay as well or as certainly as it did in olden times. With effort, you can leverage your educational edge over your lifetime. This will make you a high-net-worth investor even if you never inherit a dime. Conversely, if you pass four or five years studying dance at a private college, you will leave school with such a crushing weight of indefeasible debt that you will have effectively made yourself an indentured servant to Sallie Mae for life. If you are a parent about to send your child full freight to a middling private college, my guess is that your child will end up richer if you spent the same quarter-million dollars buying her a 7-Eleven franchise instead. She will learn the equivalent of a Columbia MBA in six months.

Statistics teach us how to avoid poverty: finish high school, take any legitimate job, work full time, year-round, and avoid having children until after you are married. This is also the way to become well-off: you do the same things, only you do them more. More education, more work, and more postponed gratification. Of course, we all know rich people whose lives haven't followed this template. Luck plays a tremendous role. That is all the more reason to stack the deck in your favor.

When you first enter the labor market, there often follows a period of trial and error where you try on different hats until you find the one you like. A timeless rule for anyone starting a career comes from Warren Buffett's Pentium coprocessor Charlie Munger: "Work like you own the place." Even if you are a lowly employee, act as if it's your family business. Once you find your niche, you will rise and acquire seniority and be compensated accordingly.

If you are presently affluent, all this is past and prologue. Now the question is: how do you stay on track?

LEAVE YOURSELF AN OUT

In the 1950s TV show *Father Knows Best*, Jim Anderson worked 9-to-5 as an insurance agent and supported his family of five in U.S. upper-middle-class splendor. Your world isn't like that. Today's Jim Anderson gets early retirement. First, some sharp young kid at the office steals his accounts. Then his wife leaves him and his children become juvenile delinquents. In other words, your job situation is going to be unstable. Burnish your human capital at every point: maintaining your education, your personal skills, your appearance, your integrity, and your connections at a high level. A fast-changing world rewards those who are nimble and quick. When you find a good gig, it is tempting to settle in for the duration. However, capitalism's dance of creative destruction assures that good gigs do not last forever. They last for a while, and then they go away.

When learning to drive, you are admonished to always "leave yourself an out." The same applies to careers. I have known many people who had a great Plan A that fell apart when the business changed beneath their feet. They had no Plan B, so they ended up in Plan 9 from Outer Space.

GET AND STAY MARRIED

Divorce is fantastically expensive. Divorce may be necessary for your emotional well-being, but it will set you back a decade in your quest for affluence.

If you can locate a sensible person with whom to contract a matrimonial alliance, so much the better. Ideally, this person is gainfully employed and has experience in the real world working full time at a real job. S/he should be careful with money and not have an air of entitlement. At a minimum, s/he should be aware that people who become affluent typically do not punch a clock, and should be prepared to be supportive rather than complaining about how hard you work.

MAKE SURE YOU CAN AFFORD YOUR CHILDREN

Never mind the cost of raising the average child ($900,000 to age 22, according to the latest study); you are affluent—what is it going to cost to raise *your* uberchild? Private schools? Riding lessons? World-class orthodontia? Broadening travel? Graduate school? A storybook wedding fit for a bridal magazine? These things are not cheap. You might think nothing of denying yourself some gewgaw, but it is harder to deny your children. As a parent, there is nothing easier than saying, "Yes." You will be shocked at the new math when you live in a power zip code and baby makes three. Kindergarten tuition at the Horace Mann School in Manhattan now costs $39,100 per year—more than any tuition in the Ivy League. In thirteen years these parents will exclaim, "Great news, honey: Daphne got into Princeton. Now we can really start saving!"

LIVE WITHIN YOUR MEANS

"Annual income twenty pounds, annual expenditure nineteen six, result happiness. Annual income twenty pounds, annual expenditure twenty pounds ought and six, result misery." Charles Dickens got this right. In a world afloat on credit cards, overspending is painless. A high-profile, high-consumption lifestyle will lead to a life of quiet desperation even if it is (temporarily) fueled by a fat salary or two. This happens by default unless you take countermeasures.

The other relevant quote comes from Adam Smith: "With the greater part of rich people, the chief enjoyment of riches consists in the parade of riches." Let someone else keep up with the Joneses.

They're miserable enough anyway trying to stay ahead of the Smiths. Being a show-off doesn't make people like you; it makes people hate you. If you use money to stimulate envy in others by buying high-status possessions to project an aura of wealth, it will be impossible for you to acquire the real wealth you will need to retire comfortably.

People benchmark their spending by looking over their shoulders. When your peers are living beyond their means (as yours almost certainly are), this creates a dangerous feedback loop. Seeing how people live on TV shows and commercials is another faux benchmark. Then, we presume that we are entitled to automatically upgrade our lifestyles as we get older, but this is false. We only can live according to what we can afford, taking into account our present and future liabilities. Once you have your retirement and all the other looming big-ticket items covered, live it up. Buy yourself a bag of chips.

The famous value investor Benjamin Graham wrote in his memoirs that instead of slipping into an extravagant way of life (as he had done), "the true key to material happiness lay in a modest standard of living which could be achieved with little difficulty under almost all economic conditions." During the downturn of 2008, I had several friends who lost their homes—and these were far nicer homes than my own tar-paper shack. It was agonizing to watch. As Charlie Munger said, if you have a $2,000 monthly mortgage payment, Grandma can help. If you have a $20,000 monthly mortgage payment, no one can help. Losing your home vs. not losing your home—that is the difference maintaining a margin of safety in your personal finances can make.

If you earn $100,000 a year, you know how to budget your spending. But if you earn $5,000,000 a year, it paradoxically becomes harder. In this rarefied ether, where the amounts go beyond what we can count on our fingers and toes, we tend to spitball our spending and borrowing in relation to our income and saving, all of which seem like abstractions, and then in a downturn everything can come crashing down.

SAVE

"Save"—the sum of all financial planning wisdom in one word. Unless you are an accredited poor person, it is unlikely that the state will do much to support you. With vast unfunded liabilities gaping before it like the Grand Canyon, the government will pick your pockets every chance it gets and toss your money into the open maw. Your lifestyle might be pretty swell right now while you have a job, but what happens when that train stops? You will need the equivalent of Scrooge McDuck's money bin to see you through 30 or 40 years of retirement. That day is coming, ready or not. Under the circumstances, it is scarcely possible to have enough savings. The mistake of saving too much is no error at all compared to the prospect of being old and destitute.

Because gambling is fun and saving is not, people like to speculate with their investments and skip the saving part. This doesn't work. It is far more prudent to hit upon a sensible program for investing and then work like Sisyphus to fund it. The pretty good formula you follow for decades beats the ingenious scheme that might work for a few years if you're lucky, which you're probably not.

SAVE EARLY

Young people have thousands of uses impatiently waiting for their extra dollar: rent, clothes, car, drinks, restaurants, concerts, travel… everything. No wonder advertisers are so eager to recruit them, and banks to pack credit cards into their wallets. While a lot of this outlay seems frivolous, and in fact is frivolous, it has a subtext: landing a spouse. These dollars have an extremely high price, though, because every dollar that flies away when we are young is a dollar not invested in stocks for the long run.

Saving and consumption are on a see-saw. Spend more today, and we will have less consumption tomorrow. Save more now, and we can consume more later. What is not obvious is that the fulcrum is not in the middle of this see-saw. Saving a little more early on levers us to be able to spend far more later. Conversely, spending more when we are young on carries a high price tag when we are older, because it robs our savings of the power of long-term compounding. The cost of overspending when we are young is completely invisible at the time. It only shows up when we are older and the cupboard is bare.

For the pre-affluent, this means taking full advantage of any employer 401k match, and putting as much saving from your paycheck as possible on autopilot. If you can fund a Roth IRA during your early years in the labor force, or set up a Health Savings Account that you never touch, you will thank yourself later. Parents should contribute to Roth IRAs on behalf of their working teens, if any such teens still exist.

PLAN

As the Cheshire cat advised Alice, if you don't care which way you go, any road will take you there. This insight has been knit into a sampler by the baby boom generation.

To do better than a random walk, you need to figure out where you want to go (by the time you retire), and then backfigure how you are going to get there. This way, you will be on a track instead of a pinball getting knocked around.

It is possible to generate a more sophisticated financial plan than simply to save every penny you can. Putting this blueprint together will entail searching your financial records for W-2s, as well as those annual letters from Social Security, mortgage receipts, brokerage statements, etc. It all has to be entered into a computer, either by you or someone you hire to do it for you. You will have to speculate about your future earnings and expenses. The computer will also make certain assumptions about inflation, tax rates, and investment returns. You will end up with a 50-page report full of colorful charts and graphs along with a lot of filler.

Is this financial plan a crystal ball? No. Is it preferable to having no plan? Absolutely. The exercise forces you to look at your life as a whole and face the glaring deficiencies on the horizon. Given the indeterminacy of many important inputs, it cannot be more than a rough guide. It can steer you in the right direction and highlight the challenges ahead. This beats pretending they don't exist. Denial here, as everywhere in finance, is expensive. If you want your life to be solvent, you have to get out of denial.

You can do this yourself using a software tool called *ESPlanner*, the brainchild of Boston University economist Larry Kotlikoff. This is not some simple app where you punch in your birth date and a horoscope pops up. You will devote a weekend to gathering and entering data, running reports, troubleshooting, re-running reports, and shaping it to model your life. For an extra hundred dollars they will consult with you to make sure you put it together correctly. This is money well spent if you are a do-it-yourselfer.

The alternative is to hire someone to do this for you. You will still have to do all the information-gathering, since your planner will ask you the same questions about your income, children, retirement, special expenditures, Social Security, etc. He will keep you on track and guide you through the process. Whom should you hire? There are a couple of qualifications to look for. First, this person should have the Certified Financial Planner certification (CFP for short). They have a website, www.plannersearch.org, which will cheerfully refer you to a CFP in your own backyard. While any CFP might be expected to have a general knowledge of all aspects of the field, there are significant differences in how good they are, as you would expect. Second, they should use widely deployed software like *MoneyGuide Pro*, *eMoney*, *Naviplan*, etc. This will give you the benefit of the consensus thinking on your financial planning questions.

Whatever you do, do not sit down with someone at a bank or a brokerage house or insurance office or retail financial service firm to puzzle out your financial future. All they will do is sell you the special of the day—and make you the catch of the day. Your problem will be subordinate to their solution. Nor should you assume that someone who has the CFP credential is a financial planner. Nearly all CFPs are actually asset managers, and no wonder—it pays more. The financial plan is the carrot to lure you in and close the deal. What they really are selling is asset management for, say, 1 percent of your assets per year. Many dispense with the financial plan altogether, which is just a loss leader as far as they are concerned.

The Garrett Planning Network (www.garrettplanningnet work.com) has a network of financial planners who will create a stand-alone financial plan for you for a fee. A plan will cost anywhere from five hundred up to several thousand dollars, depending on how complicated your life is and what questions you want answered. This would be an avenue worth exploring. Specify up front that all you are interested in is a financial plan and not asset management.

Once a plan exists, it should be updated as your life changes. You can use it to address the black-and-white questions life throws your way. Should my wife quit her job? Should I buy that chalet in Aspen? What difference will it make if we move to Florida? These programs can spit out the financial implications with the push of a button. They will also update when the tax code changes, or Medicare is cut back, and so on. Your plan becomes a living document.

The difficulty with any plan is that we cannot know the future. We cannot know our future income, and we do not know what our future investment returns will be. We cannot know the future of the tax code and Social Security and Medicare and how long we will live. The fact that these particular tarot cards are missing from our deck means that we can only plug in guesstimates. The results will be perforated with tremendous uncertainty. As William Gilmore Simms said, "Economists put decimal points in their forecasts to show they have a sense of humor."

Here is what the financial plan will tell you: save. You may be affluent, but you aren't rich. You are going to require roughly 25 times your future annual income requirements salted away before you retire. That's $2,500,000 in investments for every $100,000 you want to retire on in pre-tax income (above and beyond Social Security and any pensions). See the problem? Gathering this many acorns and berries isn't going to be easy. Along the way, politicians will take every penny they can from you to buy the votes they need to stay in office. Why from you? Because you have it, and because they can. Those who save will be made to pay for all those who failed to save. This means you need to save even more.

INVEST

Saving by itself won't be enough if you keep the money in a cookie jar. You need to invest what you save. You will have to put your money at risk in capital markets in the hope that it will grow over time.

Whether you handle the investing yourself, or hire someone to do it for you, there are some widely recognized principles to guide you:

■ Control costs

While most of us devote a whole lifetime to our human capital, we apply insufficient attention to our financial capital. Then, when we do pay attention to it, we usually make things worse. As we seek the help that we unquestionably need, these helpers, like 18th century doctors, are just as likely to harm us. The simile is apt, because the prescribed treatment inevitably will entail the application of leeches.

Costs are certain; investment returns are uncertain. The less you expend on money management, the more money goes into your pocket. A percentage point or two may seem like small change, but when you consider that it compounds year after year, you will be shocked to discover the net lifetime transfer of wealth from you to the financial services industry. What with advisor fees, wrap fees, commissions, sales loads, fund management fees, bid-ask spreads on security purchases, soft dollar arrangements, marketing fees, and market impact costs (look these up if you don't believe me), expenses can easily add up to over 3 percent per year. In fact, if you do not sedulously follow a low-expense discipline, you may well be spending that much already. It is extremely hard to accumulate wealth with this big of a hole in your pocket.

Look at it from the other side. Have you ever been to a world financial capital like London or Manhattan? Perhaps you noticed all the elegant buildings and well-dressed rich people who live and eat lunch there. Ask yourself, where do they get all their money? Then, to see the surprising answer, look in the mirror.

These costs are all before taxes and inflation. Vanguard

founder John C. Bogle (the gods cry out in anguish: where is this man's Presidential Medal of Freedom?) calculated that from 1983 to 2003, when the S&P 500 Index had a nominal return of 13 percent annually, the average equity fund only returned 4.8 percent to investors after accounting for underperformance, taxes, and inflation. If you then consider that investors practice adverse market timing, buying high and selling low, most of them would have been better off keeping their money in a hole in a tree.

Obviously, you benefit by choosing low-cost investments. These are index funds, and by some miracle they also turn out to be your best long-term investments for a host of other reasons as well. More on this coming up.

Low costs also go hand-in-hand with investment simplicity, another enormously underrated virtue. Complicated financial products invariably have high fees. In fact, their impenetrability to analysis is the whole point, the camouflage used to hide the expenses. They are designed to make money for the people selling and running them. How they will be sold to you has been carefully engineered; how they will work for you is an afterthought.

One of the primary questions you have to address is, do you want to manage your own investments, or do you want to hire someone to do this for you? There are benefits and dangers either way.

The main advantage of self-management is that it is much cheaper if you do the work yourself. It keeps you close to the ground. You won't be like my friends in Hollywood who farm out every aspect of their lives that is as low-consciousness as money—investing, bill paying, etc.—until one day they wonder why it is gone.

Naturally, there is a price to self-management as well. For one thing, your advisor might be an idiot. Yes, I mean you. As Benjamin

Graham noted, it is no difficult trick to bring a great deal of energy, study, and native ability into Wall Street and to end up with losses instead of profits. One stupid mistake can cost you a lifetime of investment returns. That may not be a big deal when you are twenty-five, but when you are fifty it could mean your retirement. Consider my friend who put all his money in Internet stocks in the 1990s and made a bundle. At the start of 2000, his wife said, "Honey, this stock market makes me nervous. We're only a year away from retiring—let's sell the stocks and bank our gains." But my friend knew better: "Are you kidding? When we're making money like this?" and then proceeded to lose every dime. Now, and for the remainder of his married life, every time a new financial hardship comes their way, he is going to feel like a loser. All for doing something that felt completely natural at the time. He was cheered on by the financial media the whole way.

After meditating on the task, Columbia business professors Graham and Dodd concluded, "The investor should not be his sole consultant unless he has training and experience sufficient to qualify him to advise others professionally." If you manage your own money, you are potentially vulnerable to every crackpot investing idea that comes along. It only takes one. Even if you are wise enough to fend off these numbskull ideas, what about your spouse and kids after you're gone? An advisor can act as a buffer, protecting you from really stupid investments. It is also his job to help you stay the course when you are tempted to change directions, as happens during investment manias and panics, the most hazardous times. Jack Bogle was talking about "buy and hold" to some investment advisers, and one advisor complained, "I tell my investors to do this, and the next year, they ask what they should do, and I say, do nothing, and the third year, I say do nothing. The investor says, 'Every year, you tell me to do nothing. What do I need you for?' And I told them, 'You need me to keep you from doing anything.'"

If you decide to hire someone to manage your finances, the next question is: do you want bundled or unbundled services? The financial service profession would love to sell you bundled services. By now your accountant has probably approached you about managing your investments. Financial planners also want to manage your investments. And finally, so do bankers, insurance agents, stockbrokers, and investment advisors.

The great thing about bundled services is convenience. Everything hums along on auto-pilot. You just show up once a year and they show you some great-looking graphs. This is the preferred business model because they can tack on a 1 percent (or higher) management fee. Undoubtedly there are instances where this spins like a top. I know of firms who provide excellent service using this model. Still, I suspect they are the exceptions. Is it a bit *too* convenient?

It can be cheaper for you to purchase the services you need a la carte. Hire an accountant or a tax attorney for your taxes. Buy a financial plan separately if you need one. Hire an asset manager whose sole job is asset management. Put yourself in the center of the loop. These matters deserve your full attention.

If you buy bundled services, you should have a high level of comfort with and trust in the whole team. If you purchase financial services separately, you will do more work, but you get the advantage of having an external control, with everyone looking over their shoulders at how the next guy is doing. Your accountant can always take you aside and say, "That investment advisor is doing a lousy job: you ought to fire him" as mine did, once. But if your accountant is also your investment advisor, you are less likely to hear this.

Do you need more than one investment advisor? It depends

on what they are doing. If you hire a guy to pick small-cap value stocks, then you probably need a guy to pick large-cap value stocks, and so on for every asset class. If you hire a guy who is simply using index funds to cover broad swaths of the market, then having two guys doing the same thing would be redundant.

Do you need to use more than one custodian? If your assets are custodied someplace large, I say no. It's difficult to imagine a world where Schwab goes under but somehow Vanguard is okay, or vice versa. Even if they did, your monies are segregated and they would be transferred to whoever was still standing.

While I am wary about self-management for high net worth clients, that is not to say I have a bracing endorsement of professional management. Most advisors charge too much and deliver too little. They just want to drop you in their 60/40 humidor and never hear from you again. My pitiful reason for recommending them is that people who invest on their own usually fare even worse. You think it won't happen to you, but you are probably wrong, and it's a high-stakes gamble.

■ Diversify

You want investments that are as widely diversified as possible. Warren Buffett can make concentrated bets. You and I are not that smart. Neither is your advisor. Investors dream of beating the market through such largely futile means as picking stocks, funds, newsletters, gurus, market timing, etc., but they seriously underutilize diversification because there's nothing sexy about it. However, it is one tactic that works, and it is under your control. You want to be widely diversified, both among and within asset classes. At a minimum, this can mean numerical diversification—owning funds that themselves hold hundreds or thousands of underlying securities across all major asset classes. Diversification eschews the trap of *faux* diversification, which means owning things that sound like they are dissimilar but in fact behave the same, usually at the worst time. Why stop there? It also means spreading your investments over the decades, so you get time diversification. Finally, your investments should also be held in different types of accounts, so you get tax diversification. There will be lots about diversification in the pages ahead.

■ Manage Risk

People are always bragging about their portfolio returns, but they never mention the risks they took because they don't know what the risks are. Returns are visible; risks are the icebergs you don't see until you're Leonardo DiCaprio holding on to a plank.

In investing, you can take it for granted that there is no great return without a great risk behind it. In a world where every former physicist and engineer is running a hedge fund, opportunities for stellar returns from minor risks have been arbitraged away by the time we open our morning newspapers.

Imagine that the risk/return visibility was reversed: that it was possible to find out every minute precisely how risky your investments were just by turning on CNBC, but you only learned their returns once a year. This would immediately promote a lot of sensible and productive investing behavior. People would manage their risks diligently and then settle for the returns they could get. This is exactly correct. Unfortunately, the world works otherwise. We watch performance—the bouncing ball in front of our eyes—because of an *availability bias*. The sadder-but-wiser investor always keeps an eye on risk, especially when he cannot see it.

There are several types of risk worth mentioning. The standard measure of risk refers to your portfolio's volatility, how much it goes up and down. Everyone pooh-poohs this but it (standard deviation, to statisticians) is a surprisingly robust measure. No one has come up with any single better idea.

Another risk is your risk of running out of money, or the risk of underfunding your major goals such as retirement. You don't want to be forced into a government home when you are ninety years old.

There are other less prominent investing risks. There is the risk famously noted by H.L. Mencken that you might make less than your wife's sister's husband. Or, you might not perform as well as some benchmark, like the S&P 500 index or one of the other hundreds of benchmarks out there in benchmarkistan.

Once you are in the market, the main investment risk is that you will freak out and commit financial suicide by going to cash in the middle of a downturn. Everyone has a breaking point. A loss of fifty percent of your money? Eighty percent? You may not know it until you get there. It occurs in a world far worse than the one we live in, where faith in global financial institutions is crumbling and even the financial future of the United States may be in doubt. Short of this calamity, there is a lot you can do to control risk, as we will see.

■ Keep the long view

While you have to keep one eye on the benchmarks, you also have to maintain the long view. Most investment activity is a lot of churning that leads nowhere. If you didn't have a good idea to begin with, it's doubtful that you will come upon a better one during a panic attack. This is why it is vital to know what strategy you are following and to understand it well enough to be strapped in. Those documents you signed that warned you that investments can lose money? They weren't kidding. There is not a morning when you put money in the stock market that you can't lose twenty percent that afternoon.

This means that you have to learn to override your emotions. Your emotions are a perfect guide for what not to do in the stock market. The last thing you ever want to do is go with your gut. You want to go with your head. Your emotions will have you wanting to sell when the market is down. They will have you wanting to buy when the market is high. The market looks safest precisely when it is the most dangerous. There are plenty of people lying in wait to exploit your reckless behavior during these times.

Putting money in the stock market is not a recipe for comfort. If you feel comfortable, you don't understand the risks you are taking. The trick is to get as much expected return as you can for the level of risk you are exposing yourself to (whether you know it or not).

■ Avoid financial predators

I once factor-analyzed every rock and roll song ever written according to gender. Songs sung by boys clustered around the following themes: you're beautiful, I love you, you're everything to me, be mine, trust me. Yet the songs sung by girls had a remarkably different subtext: you broke my heart, you cheated, you lied, you rat. In the disco atom-smasher of boy-meets-girl, there appeared to be a mismatch between what was promised and what was delivered. Imagine my surprise when I found the same story in the financial services biz. The sellers were singing upbeat numbers like: astounding returns, 5 stars, big profits, no risk, trust me. Yet the buyers were all singing the blues. In both cases, the process repeats itself as a new boyfriend/advisor is found to heal the old breakup (I know he hurt you bad but you can really trust me), and the circle game starts all over again. In investing, as in romance, this runaround can be heartbreaking and expensive.

The financial services profession has a large number of smart, dedicated professionals. It also has a lot of werewolves. Unfortunately, it isn't easy to tell them apart. There even are werewolves who do not know they are werewolves. They are either incompetent or unknowingly self-serving. Economist Herbert Stein called this Milken's Law: "the constant 'me' is always greater than the variable 'U.' " Human nature being what it is, there is bound to be plenty of bad behavior in any field. In finance, though, the temptations are especially high and the consequences for those affected can be drastic.

It would be nice if there were some professional designation like "M.D." that could protect you. But there are a bewildering assortment of titles and designations in this field. If you go to the website www.finra.org, you can look up what the initials mean, which is usually not much. Chartered Financial Analysts (CFA) have the toughest test. Other things being equal, I would look for a firm that has a CFA in the chain of command overseeing asset management.

You cannot afford to overlook how your advisor is compensated. Most Registered Investment Advisors are independent and fee-based, which theoretically aligns their interests with yours. While no one is completely on your side, at least no one is paying them to sell you anything. Stockbrokers (Registered Reps), while they may sport a variety of meaningless titles on their business cards, work for commissions. They are salesmen paid to sell you a Chevrolet. They are not even obligated to hold themselves to a fiduciary standard, to put your interests first. The last thing you want is investment advice from someone working on commission. "It is not easy to get rich in Las Vegas, at Churchill Downs, or at the local Merrill Lynch office," said Nobel economist Paul Samuelson. You want the only money your financial advisor makes to come from you.

The National Association of Personal Financial Advisors (NAPFA) will happily refer you to a fee-only advisor. Despite their lofty mission, no fewer than two of its recent presidents have been investigated for kickback schemes (one for defrauding clients by secretly putting $47.5 million of client money in a start-up he founded). Several years ago, I referred someone who was looking for an advisor to this group. When I followed up to ask how it went, he said, "The guy they sent me to tried to sell me a variable annuity." This is exactly what fee-only advisors are not supposed to do: push high-margin commissioned products. This organization is a useful idea and I wish I could endorse it, but the execution leaves something to be desired.

If you are going to hire an advisor, check them out. The Securities Exchange Commission keeps updated information on all these folks at: http://www.sec.gov/investor/brokers.htm. By following the links there you can drill down to your person of interest. These filings are worth examining in detail. Look for regulatory actions against them and conflicts of interest. Look at who owns and controls their firm. It is interesting to know what your prospective advisor did before he became an advisor. You might prefer someone with a background in astrophysics to someone who was an organ grinder.

Avoid advisors who take custody of your assets (think: Bernie Madoff). You want your assets to be held at an independent custodian. Companies like Schwab, Fidelity, and TD Ameritrade spring to mind. These companies have national reputations to safeguard and don't want to do business with shady operators, so they have already done a preliminary level of due diligence on your behalf. Notice how you never read in the *Wall Street Journal* about someone suing Fidelity because an advisor ran off with his money. These firms have a salutary self-interest in seeing that that headline never appears in the papers.

Client accounts at independent custodians are always kept segregated from the custodian's own business. If Schwab were to fail tomorrow, clients with assets parked there have nothing to fear. The accounts would be transferred to another custodian. There would be some inconvenience, but no money would be lost. One of the scary details attending the downfall of Jon Corzine's MF Global was how his firm raided client accounts for $1.2 billion. Keep your money someplace big and well-known.

An independent custodian sends you monthly statements showing what's in your account. They offer online access letting you peer into the vault any time you please. If you wake up at 3:00 AM and wonder if your money is still there, you can log in and check.

As an investment advisor, I spend my day not answering the phone and ignoring e-mails. Everyone has a great idea for how I should invest my clients' money—an idea that invariably involves giving the money to them. One of the ways I add value to clients is by never talking to any of these people. I highly recommend that you do likewise. Don't take meetings with financial salesmen. If you are looking for an investment advisor, make sure you find them —don't let them find you. The people who find you will be the wrong people. They will be great at marketing and sales and have an impressive handshake and a seamless pitch. They will seem smart and act like they want to be your friends. Every investment they are promoting will have a convincing story behind it. That's okay, you don't want it or them anyway. The whole idea is not to focus on this or that specific hot investment, of which there is a bottomless supply. Individual investments only make sense insofar as they fit into your overall financial plan; they make no sense on their own. You only want to talk to people you find yourself, through your own process of due diligence. Otherwise you will end up with an expensive annuity or an illiquid limited partnership or a revolving platter of hot stock picks. Find someone who is not particularly eager to take you on as a client—someone whose idea of fun is a really good spreadsheet. Other things being equal, I would look for an advisor with access to Dimensional Funds (started by economists from the University of Chicago), since this shows they are approaching finance from an academically serious point of view. You want someone who is going to be using index funds rather than picking 5-star funds off a list and charging you 1 percent for the privilege.

Another consideration is the size of the firm. There are solos, boutiques, and mega-firms. The smaller the firm, the more it will be about you; the bigger the firm, the more it will be about them. The bigger the firm, the more your treatment will be standardized, which has both its pluses and minuses.

Don't hire anyone you can't fire. If you let your brother-in-law manage your money, and he screws it up (which he will, eventually), you are either going to have to grit your teeth and live with it to keep peace, or pull the plug and create family drama. Don't set yourself up for a situation like this. The first thing a new broker is told to do is to "harvest" his natural market. This means Mom, Dad, and everyone else in his family and all the family friends. He will say that he wants the meeting with you just to practice his pitch and get feedback. That is a lie. It will work out better for everyone if you duck this meeting.

■ Monitor your performance

Along with an independent custodian, it is nice to get performance reporting that is independent as well. Someone like Bernie Madoff could reassure his clients because he printed and mailed off his own fantasy performance reports showing everyone how well they were doing year after year. Or, as Peregrine Financial's Russell Wasendorf, Sr. wrote in his confession, "Using a combination of Photoshop, Excel, scanners, and both laser and ink jet printers, I was able to make very convincing forgeries of nearly every document that came from the Bank." I don't want to put too much emphasis on this, because many advisors do their own performance reporting using professional software packages. If they hire someone external to do it, that seems to me a slightly better model—another pair of eyeballs on the money.

One of these companies told me that an advisor had asked them how he could "edit" his performance figures. Evidently he liked to improve the numbers a bit to keep everyone happy. You want to avoid people like this. If you invest money, you are going to get bad news from time to time, and sometimes quite a lot of it. You want someone who will give it to you straight. As Warren Buffett puts it, "Good news can always wait. Bad news should be delivered immediately."

Just because you monitor your performance doesn't mean you should immediately act on this knowledge when you are underperforming. All you can control is strategy. The outcome is in the hands of the gods. Having a good strategy should lead to a good outcome over time, but there are no guarantees. As an investor, you will pass through the dark night of the soul. It can be very costly to make big shifts in direction when the market is down 25 percent and you're losing sleep wondering why you bought all these stocks in the first place. The market has cut Berkshire Hathaway's share price in half on no fewer than three occasions. There have been stretches for years when it has underperformed the market benchmarks by a wide margin. People who understood Warren Buffett's investment philosophy held on to their shares and prospered. People who only watched the benchmark without understanding what they were doing liquidated their positions, to their cost.

Focusing on performance is a shortcut that leads to disappointment. If someone posts sizzling performance numbers, we assume that there is a profound investment strategy underlying them. But it might be luck, or it might be reckless risk taking, or the data has been edited to present a misleadingly strong case. People who invest by performance numbers are chasing the train that's already left the station. They are left wondering why the returns they see are not the returns they get. Understand the strategy you are following, control the risks you are taking, and then accept the performance you receive.

What you want to avoid is getting a thick envelope of brokerage statements every quarter with no mention of your overall performance and how it stacks up against the relevant market benchmarks. This happens all the time, because the industry wants to facilitate your tendency to live in denial. It gives the money manager a license to underperform, especially via expense extraction to his parent firm. You want to be in a position to hold your manager's feet to the fire. This is even more important if you are your own money manager.

By the standards presented here, you are undoubtedly doing a lot wrong. We all are. The road to financial well-being involves chipping away at Seven Deadly Sins. Addressing them is a continuous discipline if you want to be burdened with money. Avoiding the most egregious mistakes is the best most of us can do.

1. Denial: What—me worry?
2. Not working hard in an area where you have an edge
3. Got no plan
4. Overspending/undersaving
5. Gambling instead of investing
6. Transfusing your savings to the financial services industry
7. Not staying the course in bad times.

Chapter Three: How You Invest Depends on Your Life Stage

"A substantial holding of common stocks corresponds with the traditional attitude and practice of the wealthy individual."

—Graham and Dodd, *Security Analysis*

G raham and Dodd got it right: according to the 2010 *Survey of Consumer Finances,* 90.6 percent of families in the top income decile own stocks, which comprise slightly over half their financial assets. This chapter may represent a slightly different "take" on the topic of life-stage investing than you have read before, so let me lay the groundwork with a few anecdotes from economics.

On George Burns's 90th birthday, his friends arranged to have four beautiful young women come to his house. Taken by surprise at finding them on his welcome mat, Burns reflected for a moment and said, "Girls, I'm afraid I'm not the man I once was. One of you will have to come back tomorrow."

This is what economists call *diminishing marginal utility.* The first bite of pizza tastes great. The second bite isn't quite as satisfying as the first, and so on. We eventually reach a point where we are indifferent to more.

NOT ALL DOLLARS ARE OF EQUAL VALUE

A man offers you a coin-tossing bet. If you win, he gives you $100. If you lose, you give him $100. Do you take the bet? No, you don't.

Why not? You should be indifferent. Financially, you are no better off taking it or refusing it. Yet you pass.

The reason is that you are *risk averse*. If you won the bet, you might pat yourself on the head for winning. But if you lost, you would kick yourself for losing the hundred dollars. The kick feels worse than the pat on the head feels good. Your psychological disposition follows the classic "S"-shaped curve shown in Figure 3.1.

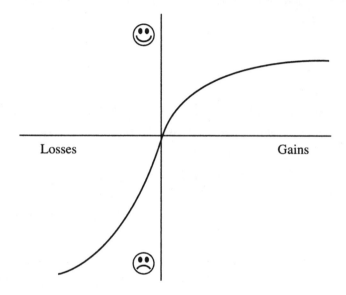

Figure 3.1

This asymmetry between wins and losses is the oldest finding in behavioral finance. Just looking at the upper right quadrant of Figure 3.1, you can see how, as your wealth increases (moving to the right), your satisfaction goes up rapidly at first, but then plateaus. Eventually, it takes a lot more money to make you any happier. Furthermore, it doesn't matter where you are on the S-shaped curve: losing always feels worse than winning feels good.

The diminishing marginal utility of your next dollar leads to your stance of *constant relative risk aversion*.

In 1974, Richard Easterline did a controversial study examining income and happiness, concluding that our national happiness had not grown commensurately with our Gross National Product. People in the U.S. today appear to be no happier than they were in the 1950s even though our country is far richer. As individuals, we quickly habituate to whatever new level of wealth we attain, and to make things worse, we constantly benchmark our well-being by looking at our neighbors. A man might feel prosperous driving home in his new Cadillac, but when his neighbor pulls up in a new Bentley, he feels like a loser.

This has implications for how you should allocate your investment portfolio.

THE FRONT NINE AND THE BACK NINE

Paul Samuelson was a brilliant economist, a fact recognized even when he was a student. Mark Kritzman tells the story of Samuelson's Harvard Ph.D. dissertation defense, that final ritual of passage for graduate students. After fielding questions from his dissertation committee, Samuelson left the room as customary so they could deliberate his fate. One of his professors turned to the others and said, "Well, do you think we passed?"

Years later, when Samuelson was a professor at M.I.T., he presented a luncheon colleague (E. Cary Brown) with a hypothetical wager. The details of the bet are lost, but it went something like this: Brown would win $200 if, upon tossing a coin, it comes up "heads"—but would lose $100 if it came up tails. Brown said the loss would be too great, even though the odds were decidedly in his favor. Then Samuelson countered: Would Brown be willing to engage in 100 of these coin tosses, such that the law of averages would lock in his edge? Brown said in that case, yes, he would.

Remember, these are two M.I.T. economics professors talking....

Samuelson went on to prove that Brown was wrong. While the law of large numbers would make Brown's loss improbable, the magnitude of his potential loss becomes greater with every toss of the coin. There is an unavoidable tradeoff between a smaller probability of a loss joined at the hip with the possibility of a large loss. If you are concerned about the size of the loss and not solely the probability of the loss, it makes no difference how many times you toss the coin. Even though the odds of your house burning down this year are remote, you still buy fire insurance, because the size of the loss would be immense.

This tradeoff implies that, other things being equal, people should not invest differently based on their time horizon. If an allocation that is 75 percent to stocks and 25 percent to bonds seems too risky to you over one year, it does not get any safer over 20 years. Whatever apportionment you decide between safe and risky assets, it should stay constant over time. If a 60 percent allocation to stocks and a 40 percent allocation to bonds is right when you are 25, it will still be right when you are 55 and when you are 85.

However, there is a missing piece. When you take all the relevant factors into account, a different allocation to equities is prescribed as you go through the Front Nine (pre-retirement) on to the Back Nine (retirement). This insight was articulated by Fischer Black in his Financial Note No. 6b, "The Time Diversification of Investments" (1968). Black writes, "The principle of time diversification is this: just as an investor should spread his investments across different securities to minimize the risk associated with a given expected return, so also should the investor spread his investments across different time intervals to minimize the risk associated with a given expected return." Harvard economists Ian Ayres and Barry Nalebuff have recently spelled out the implications of Black's formula (which prefigured his later Black-Scholes options pricing formula).

Figure 3.2 shows a graph of your financial net worth over your lifetime. It is a familiar bell-shaped curve.

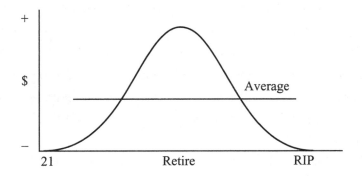

Figure 3.2

When you start work in your twenties, you have little if anything in the way of financial assets (you might even have had negative financial assets in the form of student loans). As the years pass—as we move to the right on the bottom axis—through saving and investing, your wealth grows. Your nest egg reaches its zenith when you retire (in the middle). Thereafter, you go from the "accumulation" phase to the "decumulation" phase as you consume your wealth throughout retirement. By checkout time, you might have very little left, or, if you check out early, the remainder goes into your estate.

That horizontal line drawn across the middle of the bell? That's your average lifetime financial wealth, the bell-curve flattened out.

Assume that you select a 60/40 stock/bond portfolio. Let's also posit that your average lifetime wealth is $1,000,000 (to pick a round number). If your average portfolio will be $1,000,000, and your risk aversion puts you at 60/40, this means on average throughout your life you would want to keep $600,000 in stocks and $400,000 in bonds.

What's the problem? Well, you do nothing of the sort. At age 30, with savings of $30,000, you have 60 percent or $18,000 in stocks. At age 65, with $2,000,000 in savings, at that same percentage, you have $1,200,000 in stocks. At age 90, with $30,000 in savings, you have $18,000 in stocks. The percentage exposure has remained constant, but so what? You don't eat percentage. Your absolute dollar exposure to stocks has fluctuated wildly. This adds a new risk.

In other words, you lack Black's time diversification. Instead of having your lifetime ideal measure of $600,000 exposed to the stock market over 75 years, the big money is really only in stocks over the hump—the middle years, from roughly age 55 to 75. That's making a big bet on one 20-year roll of the dice. You might get 18 percent mean annual returns or you might get 3 percent annual returns over that period, with your retirement hanging in the balance. Even worse, there is no law that says you cannot get a *negative* return. This point will not need belaboring to an audience who has recently seen a negative 20 percent total return to the S&P 500 index over a 12-year period. If you believe in stocks for the long run, then you want to be meaningfully exposed to stocks for the long run, and should not have a trivial exposure for a short run (young adulthood) followed by overexposure for a short run (middle age) followed by underexposure for a short run (retirement). You don't want to bet 90 percent of your lifetime investment returns on one twenty-year stretch.

Paradoxically, your constant relative risk aversion prescribes changing your asset class exposure, once your lifetime financial capital is taken into account. Ayres and Nalebuff think it should start off at 200 percent equities (using leverage to get there) early in your career, and then flatten out at 40 percent as retirement nears.

By a fortuitous coincidence, this is similar to what economists Gomes, Kotlikoff, and Viceira found in their 2008 paper on "Optimal Life-Cycle Investing." When human capital is taken into account, the computer model recommends an allocation to equities like the "smile" allocation shown in Figure 3.3. It is essentially the inverse of the human capital curve shown in Figure 3.2. Note how their allocation to stocks jumps up in the middle. This is when Social Security kicks in. Social Security is like an inflation-indexed bond, so it allows you to make a correspondingly higher allocation to equities once you start receiving it.

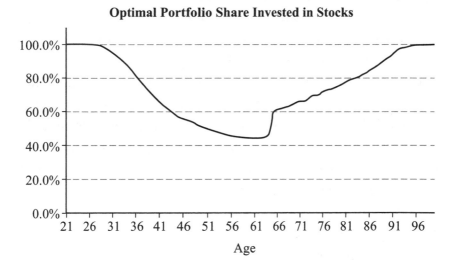

Optimal Portfolio Share Invested in Stocks

Figure 3.3

The ratio goes from 100 percent equities in your twenties and thirties down to about 45 percent equities near retirement, and from there ascends upwards towards 100 percent equities once more. The idea is to invest more aggressively when you have fewer assets, and invest more conservatively when you have more assets.

Can young people and old people really afford to invest with an extremely high equity allocation?

YOUNG AND OLD

When you are young, you have three balls in the air. First, there is your labor and the money you will take from it over your lifetime. Then there is your savings rate and how much money you can make stick to your fingers from paycheck to paycheck. Finally, there is your investment portfolio.

When you put all these together, you have the flexibility to invest your portfolio aggressively. And, hallelujah, this is exactly what financial advisors recommend, although perhaps not fully appreciating why. Even if your investment portfolio falls apart, even if you put all your money into the stock market in terrible years like 1929 or 2007, it's not a catastrophe. You still have the other two legs of the stool propping you up: your ability to work and your ability to save. In fact, these are far more momentous determinants of your lifetime net worth than the balance on your brokerage statement at this point. You have both a Plan B and a Plan C: you can work more, you can consume less, you can save more. Unlike your stock returns, these are variables under your personal control. It's not that you have more time to invest that lets you invest more aggressively at the outset (although probably that will help); it's that you have other assets as well.

When you are old, it's a different story. The prevailing investment counsel is to hold your age in bonds: if you are 80, your portfolio should be 20 percent stocks and 80 percent bonds, and so on. This is wrong. Why would you choose to augment portfolio risk precisely when you would be the most vulnerable and the least able to work? The bittersweet answer is because with every page you tear off the calendar, your portfolio has that much less far it has to carry you. As time compresses, with an ever-shortening period over which your nest egg needs to sustain you, your allocation to stocks can increase at the same level of payout (or, alternatively, your payout can increase at the same level of stocks).

STARTING OUT

In young adulthood, there are numerous practical issues to be considered.

- No investment program is going to be as lucrative as paying off revolving credit card debt.

- You will want to accumulate a cash reserve fund to carry you through several months of living expenses in case you are laid off.

- You also may want to save for the down payment on a house. This should be kept in cash or some near-cash equivalent.

- If you are planning on having more than one child, it will almost certainly be worthwhile to buy a house in a good neighborhood with a still-functioning public school system. Your property taxes will be less than two private school tuitions.

- Spending time worrying about your $10,000 investment portfolio is not a good return on investment, nor will you be able to afford to hire a money manager. Your marginal hour is far better ploughed back into your human capital, where it pays enormous dividends. You want to follow a low expense (indexed) investment program that requires almost no tending on your part. When your friends tell you how much money they are making with their stock picks, be polite and do not laugh in their faces.

■ Another smart use of your marginal hour is in finding and landing a suitable spouse. Rock'n'roll Romeos looking for their juke box Juliets typically want a lingerie model from Victoria's Secret. However, you also need to address these questions: Does this person seem like s/he would be a good mother/father? What would my parents think? How much insanity is there in the family? Can I afford the psychodrama this relationship generates?

■ In practice, the bulk of your long-term investments in early- to mid-adulthood will be inside your 401k plan. These plans amount to a disgraceful looting of the American worker by the financial services industry, all with the willing collusion of witless employers. The intelligent move for most young workers will be to review the plan offerings with a magnifying glass, find the stock fund with the lowest expense ratio, and then put all your contributions into that fund. By the way, it will be the S&P 500 Index fund. Ignore the fancy names and the performance history and the rest of the boilerplate, which can cause brain damage. Select the stock index fund.

■ If your total 401k fees are above 2 percent, then just fund it enough to capture your employer match, if any. Take the money you otherwise would have put into the 401k and invest it in a brokerage account at Vanguard or Fidelity or Schwab, where they will set up a systematic investment/withdrawal plan from your checking account.

■ Money outside of your 401k can be invested in high-beta stocks, such as small company and value stocks, using index funds that target these market segments. See the next chapters for more on this.

MID-CAREER CAREENING

By your mid-thirties, you can drop your equity allocation to 80%. To get there, put 20 percent of your 401k into the cheapest bond fund you can find. It will be the index fund that tracks the Barclay's Aggregate Bond index.

At forty, you should consider resetting your overall investment portfolio to something like the canonical 60/40 allocation. By now you probably have some outside holdings as well, so you have to weigh where to park your assets for the greatest tax efficiency. Since bonds are less tax efficient than stocks (even at today's meager yields), keep your bond allocation in a tax-deferred account like your 401k and use your taxable accounts for your stocks.

Do you have kids? Do you want them to go to college? Then you need to open a 529 plan the moment they are born and fund it to the limit you can afford. Encourage your relatives to make donations to your plan in lieu of sending cute baby outfits. While a 529 plan can count against you slightly when it comes to need-based financial aid, don't worry—you won't qualify for need-based financial aid anyway.

By fifty, other things being equal, you want your overall portfolio to be in the 50/50 stock/bond range. If at any spot on the front 9 you realize that you have 20 times your projected annual retirement income already accumulated in assets (net of Social Security), it is time to drop to a conservative investment posture, say 40/60. This might apply to anyone who comes into money along the way, or someone who has been able to save a lot, or who has earned exceptional investment returns. There is no point continuing to take a lot of risk once you have won the race.

LATE-CAREER, PRE-RETIREMENT

Now you are managing a sizeable portfolio of assets. Because a mistake here can be costly, this is a good time to hire a financial advisor. You will be looking at investing across a half-dozen asset classes, and the odds are that you do not have the expertise and the temperament to manage this alongside everything else you are doing.

Worse, from a retirement income perspective, a major wipeout of your portfolio at this point will affect your income for the balance of your life. Once you are within five years of retirement, your portfolio should reach its perigee: about 40/60 stocks/bonds. If you haven't already, this is also a time to consider alternatives: hedge fund strategies, gold, anything that will not topple in the event of a market crash.

In theory, your investments should be radically diversified from day one, but in practice, this is not possible. Funds have minimums. Advisors have minimums. Early in life, you want a mindless, automatic, all-equity, high-beta investment in order to improve your diversification across time, so that your lifetime investment returns are not compressed into one or two mid-life decades. Now, holding a substantial portfolio, you need major diversification across asset classes. When you were young, you wanted to get the maximum returns. Now, risk management moves to the forefront, and low volatility stocks move to the top of your shopping list. More on this soon.

Meanwhile, let us hope that your parents are still in good health and that they have made adequate provision for themselves, fortified with long-term care insurance. If you have a daughter who seeks to plight her troth, either pay her to elope, or hold a fashionable international "destination" wedding in Thule, Greenland. Fish are plentiful, and a single WWII Quonset hut can hold everyone who RSVPs while doubling as a barracks. Invite everyone you know—the cost will be surprisingly affordable.

RETIREMENT

Keep your asset allocation conservative for the first ten years after you retire, and then you can start to ramp up your stock holdings. By the time you are in your 80s, you can hold your age in stocks, maintaining this posture up until age 100, when you level off (by which I mean, your stock portfolio levels off at 100 percent). Alternatively, you keep the equities level and cash in the extra risk in the form of a higher withdrawal during later retirement.

Has anyone noticed? The financial services industry is bankrupt when it comes to ideas for retirees. The whiz kids all work in finance, and yet they've come up with nothing.

One idea was the target date mutual fund: a fund that could suit all comers, ratcheting down volatility over time. Wall Street loved this idea. It allowed an investment firm to trap all of your assets in a single fund-of-funds, and then farm out your money to the expensive, mediocre funds their firms offered inside the wrapper. No wonder the performance of these funds has been so dismal.

No two target date funds are alike. This telegraphs that investment allocation is not an exact science. Ben and I wrote about this problem in *Barron's* years ago, and nothing has changed since. They all performed miserably during the financial crisis. In fact, target-date mutual funds get both tails of the life cycle wrong. They are too timid in the early years of the accumulation phase, and once retirement is reached they shift to an unchanging steady-state income model. The target date funds that my friend Geoff Considine manages at FolioInvesting are excellent, but then they aren't available in your 401k, are they?

Another idea is to annuitize your portfolio. This at least has the advantage of allowing you to pool your longevity risk. When you save for retirement by yourself, you have to plan for your maximum life expectancy. When you buy an annuity, you join a risk pool: those who die young pay for those who live long. The insurance company peels itself off a generous fee for the arduous job of cutting the checks and putting them in the mail.

This payout is not going to be the stuff of your caviar dreams. First, you need to buy a joint-and-survivor policy, so your spouse will be supported after your demise. Second, you need to get an inflation-adjustment rider, or the whole thing risks become worthless. Third, you need to have a deep faith in the insurance company. If they fail, your state may backstop them, but only up to a limit that will be far less than what you need, assuming that your state decides to live up to its financial obligations in an environment where even your insurance company has failed. Just for chuckles, I looked up a quote today for a million dollar inflation-adjusted joint-and-survivor annuity for a 65-year-old couple. It turns out that the company will pay them an inflation-adjusted $35,944 a year for the rest of their lives. Remember that the million dollars is completely atomized into periodic payouts by this transaction. This is about four thousand dollars less than you would withdraw following the supposedly safe "4 percent" withdrawal rate popularized by William Bengen in 1994, where—by the way—you also get to keep any remaining principal.

Astonishingly, there are still retirement experts who advise you to put all your nest egg into inflation-indexed bonds. As of this writing, 10-year TIPS pay a yield of…negative 0.69 percent. You have to pay the government to take your money and give it back to you. Let's be generous and assume you use your million dollars to buy a TIPS ladder spread out over 30 years at 0 percent interest. That's the same as taking $33,333 a year in today's dollars, again with your principal annihilated. P.S. This assumes that you trust that government's calculation of the Consumer Price Index will not be politically jiggered over the next thirty years, and that your considerable outlays for health care will not rise faster than inflation in general. Yet this option is often touted as being completely safe.

Sometimes it is recommended that people use annuities to cover their core expenses in retirement, and then invest the surplus for fun and profit. Good luck. With annuity payouts this low, the only people this works for are people who are so well-off they don't need to bother with annuities in the first place.

Another idea is the reverse mortgage. This is like an annuity, except they seize your house in the end, and the payout is small, and the fees are high, and if you ever need to vacate your house, you kiss the house goodbye right then. Fortunately, neighborhoods never go downhill, and old people never get sick and have to leave their homes. Oh, wait a minute—they do. Never mind.

I almost forgot to mention the defined payout fund. This is a fund that will give you the same dollars every month, no matter how the net asset value fares. If the fund does poorly, they pay you back with…your own principal, even if it means unloading your assets at the worst possible time (which it would). If the fund runs out of money when you are 85 and you still have a few years to live, that's too bad. The steady payout narcotizes owners to underlying problems.

The latest deep thinking from the insurance industry is longevity insurance. This product looks suspiciously like a re-gifted deferred income annuity. You give them money today in exchange for a policy that pays off if you live past a certain age. For example, if a 60-year-old male gives a company $50,000 today, they promise to pay him $38,369 a year for the rest of his life once he turns 85. The problem is, these are nominal dollars, which means under conditions of average inflation it would purchase what $19,000 does today. If we have high inflation, the policy could be nearly worthless. Remember that some policies that advertise themselves as "inflation-protected" actually mean they can have an annual 3 percent step up. They will not protect you if we have a few years of 15 percent inflation. Current interest rates make these policies a horrible deal. You would be better off just putting your money in Treasury Inflation Protected Bonds and not touching it for 25 years. Maybe someday you will be able to buy direct an inflation-indexed, joint-and-survivor, deferred income annuity from an AAA-rated firm with a compelling payout, but not today and maybe not ever.

All of these ideas (other than buying TIPS directly from the U.S. Treasury) are profitable for the financial services industry, but I don't see what they do for you. They are for people who have run out of other, better options and have nowhere else to go. Even the prospect of buying a TIPS ladder, which locks in a net loss at today's interest rates, does not feel safe. None of these ideas improves on the conventional wisdom of just withdrawing 4 percent annually and crossing your fingers, unfortunately for us all.

FUTURE SHOCK

Imagine that you and your spouse retire at age 65. You can't plan on living to your average age; you have to plan for your maximum age, and well-educated, affluent people like you tend to be long-lived. If you look at a joint longevity calculator, you will see that one of you has a 10 percent chance of living to age 95 and a 5 percent chance of living to age 99. These protracted withdrawal time frames stress an investment portfolio. Remember, this supposes you are both 65.

Two men were talking in the locker room of their club. One said, "Did you see my new bride? She's quite a looker." His friend responded, "Yes, but she's 25 years old, and you're 60. How did you get her to marry you? "

"I lied about my age."

"How so?"

"I told her I was 90."

Heaven help you if you are the breadwinner and have married someone young. Take your vitamins. You simply can't afford to stop working and die.

Planners and advisors like to make projections showing that there will be little chance of your running out of money before you run out of life. But there is little sense in planning for a 95 percent portfolio success rate at age 100. That would leave you with a 0.25 percent chance of outliving your savings (.05 chance of living past age 95 times a .05 chance of running out of money past that period). To think that we can plan for such intangibles as longevity and portfolio risk to that degree of precision 35 years out is laughable.

All these calculations presuppose a continuity of social, political, and economic institutions that are highly vulnerable to the cunning of history. Given the crimes and follies strewn throughout historical record, investment author William Bernstein argues that planning for any estimate of long-term financial success beyond 80 percent is fairly meaningless.

If I plug the numbers into a Monte Carlo simulator, and solve for an 80 percent longevity estimate and an 80 percent portfolio success estimate, I get an initial portfolio withdrawal rate of 4.8 percent when using a globally indexed 60/40 portfolio for the 65-year-old couple. If we think we will cheat history and so want to plan for 90 percent longevity and 90 percent portfolio success, the initial withdrawal rate drops to 4 percent. This implies a 1 percent chance of running out of money before running out of longevity (10 percent longevity risk times 10 percent portfolio risk). My only point is that these factors should be planned in parallel, to the extent that they can be planned at all.

There is inescapably a great deal of pseudo precision surrounding even the most carefully drawn safe withdrawal rate estimates. If you have $25 million dollars to invest at age 65 and a lifestyle that costs $1 million a year, you will still be living with uncertainty. In fact, if you have $25 million dollars to invest at age 65 and a lifestyle that costs $100 a year, you will still be living with uncertainty. That's why it's called "the future."

THE COUNTRY CLUB PORTFOLIO

If you are fortunate enough to have a large nest egg relative to your lifestyle expenses (either because your nest egg is large or your expenses are small), then a different set of investment rules apply. Unfortunately, not many people will qualify for this because by some law of nature our lifestyles get upgraded along with our incomes, and usually a little faster. If you can live forever on three percent of your assets, perhaps on the coupons from your bonds and the dividends from your stocks, then your portfolio can last indefinitely. You have a considerable amount of freedom and leisure at your disposal. You are in a far more fortunate position than the person who may have a higher income but who is nothing more than a lifestyle wage-slave. There is no "Front Nine" or "Back Nine" strategy; you are already living on the fairway.

Under this paradigm, you likely will set an asset allocation guided by your personal risk preference and maintain it indefinitely. The task is to efficiently allocate your assets so that you stabilize your current inflation-adjusted, after-tax income and minimize the risk of a significant drawdown that would expel you from Park Place and put you back on Baltic Avenue.

One way of looking at this is to mentally divide the family sock into two compartments. One would be for your use for the rest of your life. Break out that amount and invest it according to the principles sketched above. The remainder is an investment for future generations. With the appropriate estate planning steps in place, this money would be invested with stewardship for your heirs and charities. At least, that is how it would look under an X-ray. In practice, it would be one larger portfolio (read on), and you would take an allowance every year to keep you in Christmas crackers.

This is the general plan. Now we have to tailor it to fit your life.

Chapter Four: How You Invest Depends on Who You Are

"The dialectician is the man who sees things as a whole."
—Plato

The central metaphor of modern life has been *personalization*. Over the last half-century, the marketplace has striven to exquisitely customize its offerings to your unique tastes and preferences. A milestone was the launch of the Ford Mustang in 1964—a stripped-down car designed to be ordered from the factory with a long list of options to make it "your" Mustang. Today this trend reaches its apotheosis at places like Starbucks and websites like Facebook. Everything is about you, you, you.

In the financial services industry, this has resulted in a proliferation of mutual funds and exchange-traded funds to meet every conceivable investor interest—such that there are more funds than there are individual stocks. But this is only a transitional phase.

In the future, these mutual funds will be dinosaurs. In fact, most of them already are—they just don't know it yet. The mutual fund will be replaced by the personal fund. You will hold one fund: Fund U. It will not be exactly like anyone else's. It will be uniquely computer-optimized to your personal ecosystem, taking into account your age, life expectancy, life-stage, employment, residence, geography, tax profile, appetite for risk, concentrated holdings, employee stock options, total indebtedness, and your personal goals.

It will fit like a glove. While the mutual fund was supposed to neutralize all but market risk, the personal fund will diversify personal risk. This is the opposite of what many people do today, such as when they double down on their personal risk by investing in their own company stock. The personal fund will try to cancel out your overexposure to your job. It will compare your profile to econometric factors and try to hedge your exposure to risks in the changing economy. It will change when you change, when the market changes, and when the economy changes, automatically adjusting itself along a number of dimensions—including volatility—in real-time. It will be far from perfect, but it will represent a significant improvement for most investors. Thanks to the computer, it will be cheap—it will cost less to own than the obsolete funds we use today. It should also be more profitable. By diversifying away a lot of your idiosyncratic risk, it will let you invest more aggressively at the same level of volatility, or, alternatively, it could let you invest more conservatively at the same level of return.

This is the flying car. I only mention it to tell you how George Jetson is going to invest. However, we are chained to the present historical moment, and so we must resign ourselves to the imperfect options the financial services industry presents today. For now, everything is still all about them, them, them and not about you. This is instantly apparent from a visit to their websites. The "you" part is an inconvenience, not the center of the service model, where it should be.

A FUND U PROTOTYPE

Can something like this be done even today? I dropped by economist Michael Phillips's office at *MacroRisk Analytics* (www.macrorisk.com) and presented him with the following hypothetical. "Imagine a guy who lives in Los Angeles, where he also has $1,000,000 of equity in his home. He is 50 years old and is a senior executive in the publishing industry earning $175,000/year. Let's say he also owns a big slug of Xerox stock that Granddad left him with the proviso that it never be sold: he has been watching it go steadily down for the past decade, and his stake is presently worth about $722,000. Oh yeah—his wife inherited a Picasso pen-and-ink drawing; she thinks it's worth $200,000. He has $3,000,000 to invest."

I continued, "Now, if this guy walks into a stock broker's office, the broker will listen attentively and respond, 'I have exactly the product you need: an annuity.' If he goes to an investment advisor, the advisor will listen attentively and respond, 'After due consideration, I think you belong in our signature custom blended 60/40 portfolio.' Everyone will be taking the jigsaw piece of this guy's life and using a hammer to pound it into whatever they are selling. I want to do the opposite: build the puzzle around him so it interlocks with the contours of his pre-existing piece."

Without missing a beat, Mike turned to his computers. He pulled up data series for executive salaries in the publishing industry and calculated the present value for this fellow's future earnings. He pulled up data series for house prices in Los Angeles. He pulled up a data series for fine art prices. He pulled up a data series for Xerox. We tinkered with the model until we had his current life simulated. "Now what?" Mike asked.

"I want to generate a portfolio for him that reduces the risks inherent in his idiosyncratic personal situation."

"What universe of investments would you like to draw from?" Mike asked.

"Say, the stocks in the S&P 500 index, with no one position representing more than 10 percent of his portfolio."

Mike pushed a button, and the MacroRisk Analytics engine generated the portfolio in Table 4.1.

Table 4.1: Personal Fund for Hypothetical Investor		
Asset Name	**Symbol**	**Shares**
GOOGLE INC	GOOG	1000
INTUITIVE SURGICAL INC	ISRG	1300
WASHINGTON POST CO	WPO	1900
GRAINGER W W INC	GWW	3200
V F CORP	VFC	2900
ELECTRONIC ARTS INC	EA	100

"Why would this be better than sending him to Vanguard to buy the S&P 500 index fund?" I asked.

"The computer examined how our model of this executive's life interacts with eighteen fundamental economic factors driving our economy: inflation, interest rates, energy prices, housing starts, agricultural exports, and so on. We pay special attention to those factors where the exposure is statistically significant, because as the economy changes, which it will, those exposures are going to knock him around. The portfolio the computer came up with is designed to counterbalance those exposures, so he gets a smoother ride. If he had bought the S&P 500, the rough edges also would be smoothed considerably, down about 41 percent. However, if he bought the proposed stock portfolio, the economy's influence would have been reduced about 57 percent from where he started. That is the incremental value of custom-tailoring a portfolio in this instance: less expected volatility, which translates into a higher geometric return, which should lead to a steadier increase in overall wealth."

Interesting. Now, I'm not suggesting that this is a complete analysis. I'm demonstrating the kind of personalization that is possible today for a motivated advisor with the right tools.

This chapter will show you how you can take steps toward personalizing your portfolio while we wait for the financial services industry to catch up with the future.

RISK TOLERANCE

Let's start by talking about risk.

It is widely assumed that investors need to consult their "risk tolerance" before investing. People who have a high risk tolerance can buy risky options, the thinking goes, while people with a low risk tolerance should stick to safe investments like Treasury bills and fixed annuities. The Securities and Exchange Commission mandates that investment advisors weigh a client's risk tolerance before placing them in investments. If you have ever opened an investment account, you were asked something about your comfort level taking risk. This is for their protection, not yours.

However, psychologists question whether people actually have a stable, internal trait called "risk tolerance." Whether a person scores high or low on some *Cosmo*-style quiz designed to measure risk tolerance depends entirely on how the questions are framed. Differing scores seem to be a function of the test rather than a function of a putative internal risk-taking mental predisposition of the people taking the test.

These pencil-and-paper tests ask questions like, "My idea of a good time is (a) skydiving naked over the Kilauea volcano, or (b) browsing the stacks in the reading room of the British Museum." It is difficult to use this information to judge the correct value-at-risk for an investment portfolio. It's cute, but it doesn't connect with the job it is supposed to do.

People's comfort with investment volatility is dependent on their current state of mind. When the stock market is racing up, people are comfortable with volatility. They like risk and seek more. However, when the market crashes, they hate risk. There is no fixed picture.

Even if risk tolerance existed and could be measured accurately, why would it be an important factor to consult when considering how to invest? Your psychological predisposition to take or shun risk is irrelevant to the ultimate means to reach your investment objectives. This would be like a doctor saying that your psychological preference to wear or not to wear a cast should be an important factor in evaluating how to treat your broken arm. You should invest in the way that has the greatest prospect to fulfill your investment goals. That might mean taking more or less risk than you would prefer. If you are a sensitive soul who can brook no paper losses, the solution is to get a grip, not to invest "safely" if that locks in running out of money when you are old. A timid librarian might require a manly asset allocation to reach her goals. A motorcycle daredevil might need to be in bonds to reach his. The philosopher Ludwig Wittgenstein said that a gear that turns that is not connected to any other part of a machine, is not really a part of that machine. Risk tolerance is like that gear that turns, but in the end does not connect. It could more usefully be replaced by your "being old and broke" tolerance.

The problem risk tolerance was supposed to solve is that investors panic when they lose money. They dispose of their assets at a fire sale. Characteristically, these assets were acquired in great confidence during a preceding bull market, when the weather was sunny and cotton was high. Liquidating them means the investor executes a gigantic "buy high, sell low" transaction. Do this a couple of times over the span of your investing career and you will have been better off keeping your cash in a coffee can.

I often hear advisors talk about how well their clients have recovered since March 2009, and ridicule those who went bananas and sold out in panic against their advice. However, in September 2008, we were days away from global financial collapse. Had our government continued to respond with the same fecklessness that put us there in the first place, we would have been there. In that counterfactual reality, the people who went to cash would have looked smart, while those who held on could have been left with little or nothing as financial markets disintegrated all around them. We only know the right answer *post hoc*.

As individuals, we have no control over world events. We can try to make our portfolios efficient, getting the highest returns for the least amount of risk, and avoid taking more risk than is necessary or prudent. That is about all we can do. There is no micro preparation we can make that cannot be overwhelmed by larger social, political, or economic forces in the worst case.

For most high net worth clients, I take their subjective "risk tolerance" to be a revealed preference. A revealed preference is one we discover from our own behavior. A person may claim he hates cigarettes, but if he buys a pack of Marlboros at the newsstand every morning, we would say that he actually likes to smoke: his behavior reveals his inclination. By the time clients get to me, they are either already in portfolios that are as risky as they want them to be, or they are coming to me because they are dissatisfied with how risky they are and want something different. Either way, I have a direction.

There are personal factors that should be taken into account in deciding how to invest, in deciding where you want to set the dial between safe and risky assets in your asset allocation. To these we now turn.

BETA

Beta is a Greek letter that refers, in finance, to how sensitively an investment responds to the stock market. Some things are relatively unaffected. Your demand for milk, for example. The market might be up or down, even by quite a lot, but you are not going to change your consumption of milk as a result. You are not going to drink more milk if the stock market is up, and you are not going to scale back if the market is down. Milk consumption would be low beta.

On the other hand, you might be contemplating a trip to Paris. This vacation is going to be breathtakingly expensive. If the stock market is up a lot this year, you might feel justified buzzing off First Class on the 787 Dreamliner. But those escargots are not going to taste as delicious if you have to watch your portfolio plummeting in the *International Herald-Tribune*. You likely will pull the plug on the whole itinerary and wait for better times. This trip, therefore, could be called a high beta: it is very dependent on the stock market.

Beta is a concept we will return to repeatedly. Here's the idea in a nutshell: if your life is high beta, you want less beta from the stock market. If your life is largely independent of the stock market's vicissitudes, then—other things equal—you can afford to take more risk in the stock market. Moshe Milevsky wrote a book on this topic, titled *Are You a Stock or a Bond?*

The extreme case of beta testing arose for many of us in 2008. Here is how Ben and I described it in our *Little Book of Alternative Investments*:

The problem we see is that almost everything else in your life is closely linked to the stock market. Your job—and your spouse's job—for starters. When the economy is doing well, you are getting raises, promotions, the world is your oyster. Once a recession ar-

rives, though, it's time for layoffs and cutbacks. Work becomes like death row—who will get the ax next? When there is a recession, you cannot waltz across the street to your competitor. They are laying people off, too. Even if you hang on by your fingernails, it is going to be stressful, and the stress will ricochet throughout your life and your family's life. Meanwhile, your working spouse will be going through the same grinder. Life may look different on one paycheck or half a paycheck, and it definitely will look a lot different on no paycheck.

What else is happening while this is going on? Your 401(k) plan is going through the shredder. So is your company stock. Your stock options might become worthless. Your investment accounts—loaded with stock—are down and leave you with two bad choices: take greater risk by selling your bonds (if any), or sell your stocks when they are beaten down, which is equivalent to a farmer eating his cow.

At the same time, the housing market is a graveyard. It can take a long time to sell a house in the middle of a recession, which is naturally a terrible time to sell. Being forced to sell your home just to climb out of debt is a very stressful prospect. In short, everything in your life is going to be circling the drain at the same time.

Sheer poetry! Everyone is linked to the stock market, because the stock market is linked to the underlying economy. However, there are meaningful differences in how much exposure different people have.

As an investment advisor, for example, I am directly exposed to the stock market. When the market is up, clients are happy. I'm a genius. When the market is down, clients are unhappy. I'm an idiot. My income is tied to how well the market performs. My work is high beta, and this means that my personal investments should be low beta to offset this, so they don't blow up in my face like an exploding cigar during a bear market.

I have a neighbor who lives in an enormous house. In 2008 contractors started climbing over his abode like a colony of ants. They stayed for years, almost single-handedly pulling California out of the recession. He bought a Lamborghini and got a hot new girlfriend. The economy was collapsing, yet here he was living like Bruce Wayne. What was his secret?

The answer is, he is a bankruptcy attorney. He can read the newspaper every morning ghoulishly hoping for bad news. The worse the economy, the worse the stock market, the better for his business. He doesn't have low beta, he has negative beta. As an investor, this means his investments can be high beta. His labor income will be highest when his investments are performing badly, but his investments should soar precisely when he is sitting around the office playing with a yo-yo and waiting for the phone to ring. His human capital and his financial capital are on a see-saw.

What happens to your income during a recession? If it falls to a level where you have to dip into savings, that argues for a more conservative, low beta posture vis-a-vis equities. However, wages are "sticky." They do not drop with a general decline, they simply stop advancing. Employers know that if they cut wages, then they will have a large group of disgruntled employees on their hands, which is a recipe for trouble. Instead, they lay people off. The miserable ones are shown the door, while those who remain are overworked and stressed out, but grateful that they still have a job. Layoffs are a danger to employees because they are a disproportionate, all-or-nothing response. If this could happen to you, more caution is advised.

According to research by Parker and Vissing-Joregensen at Northwestern University, the beta of the top 1 percent has been increasing. In the old days when Granddad worked for Standard Oil, his emolument did not vary with the stock market. But today, when our powers are amplified by modern computers and telecommunications, those at the top quickly reap the financial consequences of their decisions. Their incomes gyrate procyclically, at a rate two to three times that of the general population. This trend is abetted by concentrated stock holdings, leverage, and a marginal propensity to consume that is greater than their income. They are like the early generation of Rothschilds, who never could tell from day to day whether they were millionaires or bankrupt.

Closely related to beta, and often confused with it, is volatility. Beta is volatility specifically tied to the stock market and the larger economy. Volatility by itself is unpredictability that may or may not connect to the stock market. If you are a swimming pool contractor, your calling is high beta, because you will sell more pools during prosperous times. If you work as a casting director, your employment may be volatile but it is not necessarily high beta. If you work as a teacher, your occupation is both low beta and low volatility. All this relates to how much risk you should take with your investments. Low beta/low volatility workers can take more risk. If you have a volatile job, you should take less investing risk, other things equal. If you have a high beta job, you should take the least risk, because the volatility will hit you at the same time it hits your portfolio.

None of this applies if you already have large savings relative to your consumption. If you have enough money safely invested to cover all your living expenses for the rest of your life, it doesn't matter if you work as a test pilot or mail carrier or if you work at all. You can invest any money beyond what you will need to live as a matter of personal preference. However, most of the affluent are not situated so fortunately.

Let's examine how these ideas apply to some garden variety high-net-worth types.

DOCTORS

Doctors are the single most likely occupation to reside in the top one percent of household earnings. Physicians should be top-drawer investors. They have high IQs, a science background, they understand statistics, and they are no-nonsense people because to them, time is money. Better still, they are used to making highly consequential risk/benefit decisions and accepting the consequences. Yet doctors are notoriously dysfunctional investors.

I once knew a doctor who invested in a race horse. At the time it was a tax dodge. The grooming, training, feeding, and boarding were tax deductions. Everywhere this doctor went he showed off pictures of his thoroughbred. All his spare time was spent at the stables and the track. A gastroenterologist by day, he lived as a country squire by night.

Then one day the horse got sick and died. That was sad. Then, the doctor discovered the overdue insurance renewal form in a stack of papers on his desk. That was really sad. He had meant to mail it in but forgot in the midst of his busy schedule. It was only a few days late. However, seeing that the horse was already dead, the insurance company declined the opportunity to renew the policy. His clever investment scheme turned into a half million dollar total write off.

Here are some theories why doctors don't invest as successfully as they should:

Doctors are overconfident. The self-assurance that works so well for them professionally trips them up when they invest. They believe that the force of their brains and personalities will let them power through any obstacle. They are accustomed to making fast decisions that are mostly correct. Investing sounds like an entertaining and highly profitable hobby. Because they're smart, they think they can win this game on their own terms. But they are prizefighters operating in a wrestling ring. They get taken and shaken down accordingly.

Doctors are busy. Simple economics dictates that they use their time practicing medicine, not with some sideline investing. They don't have the time to make a proper study of the field. Their attention is constantly being pulled in fifteen different directions. Yet the people they trade against have minds that are clear and focused like a laser.

Doctors assume that finance professionals have expertise like their own. Since doctors undergo arduous study and training to score their professional shingles, they assume that people who hold themselves out as finance professionals are masters of a similar body of knowledge. As doctors are used to telling it like it is, and not holding back with the bad news, they assume that other professionals will display the same level of honesty and plain dealing. They are unaware of the flimsiness of most professional certifications in finance, or the trivial entrance requirements to the field. Wealth managers are the "B" students. If they were "A" students, they'd be running hedge funds. Or, they'd be...doctors.

Doctors are a targeted high-risk group. Because they are still believed to have lots of money (like in the good old days), and because their contact information is easily harvested by marketers, physicians are surrounded by sharpies eager to take their money. Worse, doctors are always on the lookout for some angle where they won't have to pay taxes. Good luck. When it comes time to invest, top-of-mind awareness goes to the glossy brochure selling Florida swampland or the scheme to extract gold from seawater, not the *Financial Analysts Journal* in the library. Doctors can go from one dodgy idea to the next without ever alighting on a sensible approach that puts them in the way of making money.

I used to work in a hospital, so I have always looked up to physicians, but most serious investment advisors are not fans of having doctors as clients. They feel that doctors are impatient and have a gambler's mentality that is not conducive to long-term investing, while the fees do not adequately compensate advisors for taking on difficult clients—they'd rather let someone else have the chance. This only makes the problem worse, because these advisors are exactly the ones doctors should be using. Instead, they end up with stock brokers who churn and burn their accounts.

Physician, heal thyself! Investing, if it's done right, is going to be boring. It is going to require humility. You won't get rich overnight. You can't watch CNBC between appointments and make money trading stocks just because you had high MCAT scores. That way lies the poor house.

The silver lining is that physicians work in a field that is inherently low beta and low volatility. Unless you are a dermatologist Botoxing for Visa, the demand for medical attention is relatively constant no matter how the economy is doing. Patients may be slow to pay during tough times, they may postpone elective procedures, but doctors suffer less from macroeconomic factors than do the rest of us. If you are laid off today you can probably find identical work someplace else tomorrow. This means that, other things equal, doctors can profit from a high allocation to equities. Their lifetime net worth can be very high, provided they don't screw up the investing piece.

LAWYERS

Lawyers are smart, and they should be great investors, but their profession puts them at high-risk. Not to themselves, but to anyone investing money on their behalf. For example, a 2004 article in the *Wall Street Journal* claimed that Fisher Investments discouraged the firm's reps from signing on attorneys or anyone who had been involved as clients in a lawsuit.

Why? Because in the event of a disagreement, it's not a level playing field. An attorney has a perceived limitless ability to bring legal action against the advisor, for free. The advisor must tie up his time and his own attorney's time at $800/hour to defend himself, no matter how frivolous the complaint. The potential hit to an advisor's reputation is devastating, as would be the many sleepless nights along the way. Life is too short to risk this kind of aggravation.

I have lots of lawyers as clients, and down to a person they are terrific. However, I have never been sued. If I had, I'd undoubtedly feel differently.

What does this mean for attorneys? My recommendation would be to find the advisor you want, and then go out of your way to portray yourself as a low-risk, advisor-friendly, non-litigious type of client that you are.

As for how being an attorney affects your beta, it depends on your specialty. I have already mentioned my neighbor, the bankruptcy attorney, and how this should let him invest aggressively. There are so many areas of practice that it is impossible to generalize. You would have to consider how you held up through the downturns in 2000–2003 and 2007–2009. For the flip side, look at how you fared over the boom from 2004–2007. To the extent that your income was tied in to the larger economy, you should have less exposure to stocks, because your career itself is like a stock. You also need to consider the likelihood of your being let go, and how much difficulty you would have ramping up again. Most lawyers I know have steady employment, but my sample is probably biased. Newly minted attorneys are having difficulty finding work, which was once unheard of, but that is the world today.

On the basis of no evidence, I speculate that both doctors and lawyers are at high risk for divorce. Divorce can be a very expensive proposition for those with super-sized incomes. I also observe that both groups tend to live rich. Having undergone an extended and penurious post-graduate training, they feel entitled to buy fancy houses and cars to make up for lost time. This high consumption lifestyle is affordable so long as they keep up with the grind, but—coupled with a lifetime of sub-par investing—can leave them with little to show for it.

ENTREPRENEURS/SMALL BUSINESS OWNERS

These are the most sought-after clients: they understand business and business cycles, and they are invariably too busy with their main jobs to manage their own finances as a sidelight. The nature of the occupation dictates how the remainder of the portfolio should be positioned. If you own a few McDonald's franchises, your income is not going to depend on the state of the economy. It might even get better during a downturn. If you own a high-end sushi bar, it will fall off considerably. Reviewing how your shop survived during the recent downturns will be instructive.

That said, most small businesses are volatile and many are

high beta as well. This may not be true of your family pest control company that has been in Topeka for the past 40 years, but it is true of the futuristic graphic design studio you opened in LA three months ago on your credit cards. If your enterprise is a startup that could be adversely affected by a recession, that is like taking a highly leveraged stock position. The rest of your financial holdings should be conservative, so that you don't risk losing everything at once. I have a client who started a business at his kitchen table. For the next seven years, he held exactly one asset outside of his business and house: cash. He didn't come to me until his business was on its feet and he felt he could afford to take more risk with his investments.

The worst case is a private equity professional. Here you own a highly leveraged portfolio of companies that are themselves lottery tickets, with both your employment and your financial assets sunk into them at the same time. This individual should be extremely circumspect when approaching the stock market with his surplus capital.

CORPORATE EXECUTIVES

Executives, administrators, and managers are another group of prized clients: they understand business at a high level, but are too busy to manage their own portfolios with the care they deserve. The beta issues are the same as for the small business owner, except that their corporations are larger and less volatile. Another plus is that they are more employable. If GE lets a key executive go, there are numerous companies where he can hang his hat: he is a proven, marketable commodity. If the Jensen Family Tool & Die shop in Akron goes under, Jensen Junior will have a stigma attached to him because his skills have never been tested in the open market. This kid will have a lot of proving to do.

A Note About Executives and Their Options

Today's corporate executive should spend at least as much care considering how to manage his stock options and restricted stock as he does managing his airline miles. This is a daunting task, because the interwoven tax and investment issues are baffling. For this reason, most employees use their options as play money and execute them either when they want cash to buy something or when they see everyone else executing theirs because the stock price has been high lately. You can do better.

The idea is to maximize your lifetime wealth (return) while minimizing regret (risk). You don't want to be the guy who exercised his options for pennies when the IPO would have made him a multimillionaire, but you also don't want to be the guy who hung on to his company stock until it got delisted and now faces a six-figure tax liability with an empty checkbook. While the permutations go far beyond the scope of this book, here are some factors that impinge:

- Read your own employee stock option agreement. Do not presume your deal is just like anyone else's. Circle the passage where it mentions your options' expiration dates. You don't want to be one of the million employees Fidelity uncovered who let their in-the-money options expire.

- There are two components making up the total value of your options: their *intrinsic value* and their *time value*. Their total value is what you get from a Black-Scholes calculator. Their intrinsic value is the difference between your strike price and the stock's current price. The time value is the difference between the option's intrinsic value and its total value. You don't want to execute your options when they still have a lot of gas left in the tank in the form of time value. For guidance here, I commend to your attention the reports available from www.stockopter.com. These can form the foundation for a useful discussion with your advisor and CPA prior to making any moves.

■ The more volatile the stock, the closer you are to retirement, the less bullish you are on the stock, and the more of your net worth is concentrated in it, the sooner you should exercise.

■ It makes no sense to exercise non-qualified stock options and then hold the stock. You are already over-invested in your company through your human capital. Exercise, sell, and diversify.

Employee stock and stock options need to be considered in the context of your entire portfolio and not set to one side as if they didn't exist. I like the Quantext QPP Monte Carlo Simulator (www.quantext.com) for advisors as well as savvy do-it-yourselfers. This Excel-based tool will let you experiment with changing the mix in your outside portfolio to compensate for the distortions of a concentrated holding, including your stock options. The aim is to tune down the idiosyncratic risk and create a version of your personal fund.

WIDOWS, DIVORCEES, HEIRS

I have a nightmare. I have died, and, after a suitable period, my wife is at a cocktail party. A brylcreemed young stockbroker discreetly turns the conversation to the stock market, and in passing drops the name of some space-age investment product that pays spectacular dividends. The next day at his office, he looks over her portfolio, and says, "Yes, I see what Phil was trying to do for you. This was really the best that could be done at the time. Of course, today you could be making a lot more money…." and then in a couple of years everything is gone. Interestingly, my friend Ben has the same nightmare. The prospect of everything we worked for being eviscerated by some bloodsucker steams our clams. Yet it remains an ever-present possibility.

When you undergo a traumatic loss, the simple truth is that you are functionally insane for at least one year afterward. I tell people this all the time and they never believe me. This is a bad time to be making big moves. Under these conditions, the first thing to do when you are suddenly confronted with the responsibility of managing money is to do nothing. Let the snowflakes in your personal snow globe settle down.

I know an advisor who dealt with a woman in this situation. She was heading into rehab and wanted to make big plans for her money. He said to her, "You know what? I am going to put you in T-bills. This is all you have. You don't have any more. Let's make sure the money is there for you when your head is clearer." He kept her in T-bills for a year, and he charged her one percent for the privilege. In my humble opinion—not everyone will agree—he did well by her.

If you have new money in your life, for reasons good or bad (an inheritance, a disability settlement, a lawsuit), and you are not used to handling sums like this, there is one thing you desperately need, and that is a financial plan. You must go to an independent planner and have him run the numbers. This person is going to be important to your future. You are going to want to consult with him on an ongoing basis, before you make any big financial decisions— house, car, relocation, etc. Get his ideas on what your portfolio should look like, but do not invest with him.

Don't rush to execute the plan. Admire it like a Matisse in your living room. See how your feelings about it change with the seasons. Make some tweaks. If the sums are of an order of magnitude that is new to you, do a great deal of due diligence and find an investment advisor.

You will be amazed how everyone knows about your good fortune and wants to share the love. Children. Friends. Boyfriends/ Girlfriends. Everyone. Tell them you aren't doing anything with the money for a year, it's still tied up. Lie if you must. You will even discover that some of the people you thought were your friends really are your friends.

One question that often arises is: I just got $1,000,000 in cash. Should I invest it all at once, or dollar cost average it into the market over time?

You cannot know the best answer to this question in advance. If you invested the money in 1999 or 2006, you would have immediately lost a sizable percentage in the stock market, whether you invested it all in one day or over the course of the year. At the other extreme, if you invest $10,000 a year for the next 100 years while the remainder sits in your checking account, you are going to miss out on the stock market's upside.

The goal, here as with almost everything in life, is to minimize regret. Investment author Rick Ferri has some advice on this topic, which I will paraphrase:

■ If the size of the lump sum is 20 percent or less of your overall savings, just invest it according to your current asset allocation and be done with it.

■ What was the source of the money? If it was your own money already invested in the markets somewhere else, then reinvest it all immediately.

■ If the money came from the sale of a business or property that you owned, it was capital at risk. Invest half today and the rest over the next two years.

■ If the money came from out of the blue, then invest 40 percent now and the rest over the next three years.

I might tweak this based on how valuation levels looked in the stock market at the time. If the price/earnings ratio of the S&P 500 index were below its historical long-term mean, I would be more sanguine about investing more money sooner. If the P/E were above its long-term mean, I would be more wary—even if the stock market had been sniffing glue lately and everyone seemed extremely confident and happy.

If you are a young heir, your asset allocation will depend on the proportion of your net worth in your inheritance versus that forthcoming from your career. If you are not going to work at all, human capital is knocked out of the equation and you start with the country club portfolio described above. If you inherit two million dollars and you stand to save another two million dollars from your labor income, your initial portfolio can be more conservative, because you are starting out half-way to the finish line.

SCIENTISTS & ENGINEERS

As a group, these are among my favorite clients. Their math background means they instantly "get" what advisors try to do, which typically is to optimize the expected return/risk ratio. Often the beta and volatility of their careers is moderate to low (unless they are involved in start-ups), and they don't live large. They also tend to do well investing on their own: they don't try to be cute, they completely tune out the Wall Street blather, and focus on low-expense, long-term, index-oriented strategies.

CELEBRITIES/ATHLETES

At the other end of the continuum from scientists and engineers are celebrities and athletes. These are the worst investors of all and famously end up broke, for all the usual clichés:

- Big checks lead to a sense of omnipotence, disconnection from real life

- Grandiose self-importance, impatience with details

- Notoriously short careers

- High divorce rates

- Support for an entourage of hangers-on

- Steep fees at best/exploitation at worst from financial "advisors"

- Obligatory descent into booze, pills, and madness

- Acting as private banker to friends and family

- Entitlement to lifestyle of the rich and famous

- Loads of street smarts but no education in areas where street smarts don't work, like finance

- Busy being fabulous

- No Plan B

It only takes a few years to dissipate a large fortune. The killer combination is drugs + bad company + corrupt advisors, which seem to travel in packs like feral dogs.

One difference between athletes and celebrities is that athletes should know the clock is ticking on their careers, whereas celebrities believe they will be loved forever. Yet almost none are. Unless you ascend to the status of "legend"—Jimmy Stewart comes to mind, a few others—everyone else learns that "celebrity is obscurity biding its time," as Carrie Fisher described it.

It is difficult to tell a 20-year-old athlete who just signed a deal for $10,000,000 that he needs to make plans for a second career and in the interim live on $135,000 a year because after he pays his taxes and agent, etc., that's about all a sober accounting of his lifetime situation says he can afford, at least so far. He will squander more than $135,000 on a new car that week. (I would have done the same thing.) No wonder 78 percent of NFL players are in financial trouble within two years of retirement, and 60 percent of NBA players are in bankruptcy court within five years of leaving the basketball court.

It goes without saying that celebrities and athletes make terrible clients for conscientious financial professionals (but sensational clients for unscrupulous ones). They usually have no understanding of what is being done on their behalf and so cannot participate intelligently in the kind of collaboration that makes for the best long-term relationship. While their careers may be low beta, in that they are unlinked to the stock market, their work is so volatile that a conservative portfolio is frequently indicated as a counterweight. If the sums are staggeringly large, then aggressive investing becomes an option once their lifetime expenses are covered. The drill is to translate their human capital into financial capital on an accelerated schedule via a high savings rate. This rarely happens, because celebrities rationalize their expensive lifestyles as integral to the momentum that keeps the big show going.

Location, Location

Another factor to bear in mind in considering your asset allocation is where you live. This has two parts.

The first is your city. Some cities are inherently high beta. New York springs to mind. You might work at a corner deli, but if all your customers labor in the canyons of Lower Manhattan, you are going to suffer right beside them in an economic downturn.

Your burg may not be tied to the stock market, but if you live in a company town, your fortune will ricochet off those of the parent business. I live in Los Angeles, where nearly everyone is chained to the entertainment industry. Its box office grosses and Nielsen ratings become our own. By way of contrast, my brother lives in Washington, DC—the company town for the U.S. government. It keeps growing no matter who's in power or how the economy fares.

Part two is the question of home ownership. For the top 10 percent, this is typically about 19 percent of your net worth. This links your total capital to the regional market. Yale economist Robert Shiller describes two macro-markets for real estate in the U.S.: the coastal cities where the market follows a "boom and bust" cycle, and all the places in between where prices just keep pace with inflation. Both of these have been distorted by the recent real estate boom and depression, and it is unclear what new order will emerge. It may be that people's appetite for real estate speculation has been sated for a while. The main exception seems to be price-insensitive international arms dealers desperate to get money out of their own countries and shielded by U.S. law. These people make charming neighbors.

The principle remains: consider the beta and the volatility of the price of your residence relative to making other investments. If your home is either high beta or highly volatile, this would argue for a more conservative investment allocation elsewhere if there is any danger that you might have to liquidate your home in a downturn. This becomes more consequential the greater the value of your residence compared to everything else you own, and the greater the debt you have to service to stay in it.

YOUR PROFILE

Your career is like a bond to the extent that it provides a steady income over your lifetime. If you work for the government it can be like a government bond. If you work for a corporation, it is like a corporate bond. If you work at some high-risk enterprise, it is like a high-yield or "junk" bond, with an uncertain stream of payouts and a high risk of default. The correlations to the stock market rise with each of these gradations, which means that your overall stock exposure should lower to keep you at equilibrium.

You career interacts with your residence. The last thing you want is for everything to collapse at once. If you own a co-op on the Upper East Side of Manhattan and work on Wall Street, you would be well advised to have some nontrivial cash reserves. If you are a tenured professor at a well-upholstered school living in an upscale Victorian in a cozy Midwestern university town, you can hold a thimbleful of cash and invest your 403b plan aggressively in the stock market. Most readers will land somewhere in between.

There are several other noteworthy variables to consider in weighing how "bond-like" or "stock-like" your life is. In my neighborhood, several houses have built-in cabinets made by an out-of-work young actor named Harrison Ford. I don't know what he was paid to make cabinets, but let's say it was a market wage—perhaps $35 an hour, when he could get it. On the other hand, as an actor, he earned $20 million dollars for 12 weeks of work on a movie, plus first-dollar gross profit participation on top of that. Here is a man with a difference in orders of magnitude between what he was paid for his "Plan A" job—acting—and his "Plan B" job—carpentry.

What is that difference for you? In a world where you are let go from your trade, could you find a similar job within three weeks or three months? Might it entail a wrenching drop in salary? This increases your personal risk profile and the quantity of cash you should hold. If the timing of the risk coincides with a downturn in the economy, it increases your beta and further elevates your risk contour.

If your work is like a bond, when does the bond mature? Does your career have a mandatory retirement age, or do you work for an establishment where "early retirement" will be their first line of defense during an economic downturn when you are in your 50s and still have another 40 years of life to pay for? Do you have skills that are timeless and work in a field where the accumulated wisdom of a few gray hairs is seen as an advantage? I play guitar and would be open to tour with the Rolling Stones next summer. Yet, my phone does not ring. Mick, Keith—where are you? I fear age has become a liability—at least mine has. On the other hand, watching the stock market for decades proves to be a good thing in my day job as investment advisor. People don't want to entrust their life savings to some kid. In most fields, ageism rules (never mind what employment law says). I hope this changes with the demographic shift toward an older population. In the meantime, any trade you can ply in retirement, especially on a part-time basis, will cushion your portfolio. An undertaking that terminates at 62 is going to spin less hay into gold than one that ends at 70 or one that can be maintained indefinitely.

Related to this is the question of a pension. If you have a well-funded defined benefit pension that picks up where your career leaves off, you hold the Holy Grail. Most public pension plans are postulating investment returns above 8 percent annually to make them solvent; I wish them luck. If, like most of us, you have to rely on what you can squirrel into your 401k plus a few shekels from Social Security, it is going to be that much harder to maintain your standard of living in retirement.

Then there is the question of the debt you carry: how much and what kind. Your debt may be nominally tied to your home, your stock portfolio, your education, or your business, but it leverages everything (debt is fungible, since you could always sell one asset to pay off a loan against another asset). There is a great deal to be said for not assuming (or quickly dispatching) any debt tied to wasting assets like cars, vacations, and credit cards. After that, the question becomes how serviceable is your debt burden under worse-case scenarios? I have an old friend who left medical school with debt, walked into a bank in LaJolla, California and financed one hundred percent of the purchase price of a fancy home there—and this in the days before the collapse of lending standards. The banker made the right call: my friend was good for every nickel. Although he had no assets beyond his M.D. degree, in the event of death or disability insurance would have paid for everything, while in the normal case his labor income was more than sufficient to cover the interest expense. The problem comes when the debt burden is high and the ability to repay is variable. This scenario argues for extreme caution with outside investments, even if you are morally certain you will be a multimillionaire in three years.

Finally, a key underlying variable affecting the value of your lifelong income stream is your savings rate. Less consumption today equals more money and more freedom tomorrow. If you spend every dollar that you make, you will eventually live in penury, even if the bliss of your current hyper-consumption blinds you to this prospect. Just as some people have more flexibility than others in finding a new job, some people have more flexibility built into their savings rate. In both cases, flexibility is a cardinal virtue. If you are single, you can sleep in your parent's basement, use orange crates for furniture, and put orange crate art on your walls. You can save as much as you choose. If you are married with three kids in private schools, a handsome mortgage, and parents who require you to open a vein every month for eldercare, you have high fixed-cost overhead. Cuts can be made, but it is going to be painful, and cancelling HBO or skipping lattes will not make much difference. You have low flexibility in your savings rate, which probably was too low in the first place. Even with a steady career, the net present value of your human capital is compromised by your inability to divert it away from present consumption into savings. It risks lowering your standard of living once the music stops.

Your risk tolerance is not an inner psychological state of your comfort/discomfort with taking risk. It is a function of your financial goals, how much you have, what you do, where you live, how much you can save, how much debt you carry, as well as how much you are concerned about a big drop in your living standard after you retire.

Chapter Five: The Market Portfolio

"The real secret to investing is that there is no secret to investing."

—Seth Klarman, Baupost Group

Whatever the merits of John Maynard Keynes's *General Theory of Employment Interest and Money* (1936) as a prescription for fiscal or monetary policy, it is a humdinger of a book for investors. Not the book as a whole, but specifically Chapter Twelve: "The State of Long-Term Expectation." Lord Keynes was himself a superb investor. He managed the portfolio for King's College, Cambridge from 1924 until his death in 1946, earning an annual compound return of 12 percent over a period when the British stock market fell 15 percent. He was an economist with serious street cred as a stock picker.

INVESTMENT VS. SPECULATION

Keynes distinguishes between *investment* and *speculation*. In earlier times, these were bywords for bonds and stocks. Bonds (at least, Treasuries) were investments; stocks were speculations. Now Keynes pushes the envelope: while stocks may be speculations, some stocks are more speculative than others, and understanding this distinction is at the heart of what distinguished his annual 12 percent return from the market's overall negative 15 percent return.

Keynes begins with a dim view of our ability to predict the future:

The state of long-term expectation, upon which our decisions are based, does not solely depend, therefore, on the most probable forecast we can make. It also depends on the confidence with which we make this forecast... The outstanding fact is the extreme precariousness of the basis of knowledge on which our estimates of prospective yield have to be made. Our knowledge of the factors which will govern the yield of an investment some years hence is usually very slight and often negligible. If we speak frankly, we have to admit that our basis of knowledge for estimating the yield ten years hence of a railway, a copper mine, a textile factory, the goodwill of a patent medicine, an Atlantic liner, a building in the City of London amounts to little and sometimes to nothing; or even five years hence.

The problem for investors is compounded by the fact that the market is like a *beauty pageant*, where mobs of investors are not trying to calculate the long-term present value of cash flows from business enterprises, but instead are guessing how much other people will pay for a stock next week or next month, or maybe even thirty seconds from now. He likens the stock market to a casino.

Finally, Keynes takes note of *animal spirits*—our tendency to prefer activity over inaction, to let money burn a hole in our pockets and rush into things without making a cool estimate of probabilities. Psychological factors tend to artificially and alternately inflate and then depress stock market valuations.

A Keynesian, when confronting an investment opportunity, primarily would be interested in its yield. What is the probable payout from this investment? How reliable is it? There are big differences among enterprises along these dimensions.

Across the Atlantic, Graham and Dodd had recently said much the same thing in *Security Analysis* (1934). They defined an investment operation as "one which, upon thorough analysis, promises safety of principal and a satisfactory return. Operations not meeting these requirements are speculative." However, the value of analysis diminishes as the element of chance increases. Even with fancy mathematics, security analysis cannot make a precise determination of the value of a company, so investors need to buy stocks at a *significant discount* to their long-term *intrinsic value*, in order to have a *margin of safety*. In the short run, the stock market is a voting machine instead of a weighing machine. Since "Mr. Market" is manic-depressive, the investor's mission is to stay calm and wait for the pitch he likes.

Consider Facebook, a company that went public at a price of 38 dollars. What is the discounted present value of its future earnings? Well, there is quite a range of possibilities. If Facebook can transmute its users' personal information into advertising ammunition, the stock could be worth quite a lot. Alternatively, if Facebook fails to execute this space mission, its stock is worth considerably less. You might have a view on this question, and all views are distilled into the price, but there is still a large "x-factor" in the equation. There is a gear that is a future earnings multiplier/discounter, and everything hinges on what value we plug in here. Unfortunately, we don't know what number to use. There are only make-believe stories about the future.

In judging stories, people are reduced to the level of kindergarteners listening with a plate of milk and cookies. We judge a story to be true if it sounds true; that is, if it sounds like other stories we have known and loved, if it has a pleasing "arc," as they say in Hollywood. An infinite number of multiverses proceed from every moment in time, but stories—especially if they are vivid or alarming—focus our attention disproportionately on the one with the (un)happy ending. As Demosthenes said, "What each man wishes, that he believes to be true." Even though investments are often sold by telling a story about them, this is not a rational way to bet your life savings. This is speculation, not investment.

As an alternative to Facebook, consider Consolidated Edison, the electric utility company. It pays a dividend, so it has a known current yield. It has a proven business model: it sells electricity to 3.3 million customers in New York. It earns a profit on every kilowatt, and distributes the profits back to shareholders in the form of a large dividend. We perceive that it has paid this dividend every year since 1885 and raised it frequently along the way. Will New Yorkers want to continue to consume electricity for the foreseeable future? I predict that they will. It may be necessary to upgrade existing power plants to natural gas (or nuclear, solar, or aetheric energy), but that price will be passed along to consumers. While the future is ultimately unknowable, Con Ed's prospects appear more narrowly definable than are Facebook's.

Within the universe of stocks, companies like Con Ed are more like investments, and companies like Facebook are more like speculations. Investment looks to the past; speculation, to the future. If we were to buy a basket of companies like Con Ed, we would have a more reliable and predictable stream of income from their operations than we would from buying stocks like Facebook. Stocks with more predictable futures are often found in the utility, gaming, cosmetics, beverage, tobacco, health care, food, and waste management industries. Let me present an example from my own family history. The DeMuth family opened their first tobacco shop in the United States in 1770. The health benefits of tobacco use having been overstated, it closed in 2010. Tobacco has been a reliable business over the centuries while many other stores have come and gone.

A speculative investment is like a lottery ticket that stands to give you an inordinate payout if you are lucky, provided that you didn't overpay for it. People who are not interested in doing present value calculations of future dividend streams and then estimating the robustness of their calculations might simply want to buy Facebook because it is cool, because they wile away their hours updating their Facebook pages, because it gives them an opportunity to "like" themselves, or because at some unconscious level they believe owning Facebook makes them cool via contagious magic. Interestingly, the market is a place where two different agents can operate working past each other: on the one hand, investors looking for a stream of dividends, and on the other, speculators who don't know Cisco from Crisco gambling in a casino where their animal spirits can find release trying to guess the next winner in a beauty pageant.

THE ROAD TO DISASTER

The predicament of the affluent is that setting out to invest their money is more like walking into the Bellagio Hotel in Las Vegas than into the Booth School of Business at the University of Chicago. The financial services industry does not exist to make them rich; it exists to make itself rich by selling financial services and products. To Wall Street, those of high-net-worth are a livestock commodity: sheep to be shorn. The industry is a confidence game that offers them friendship and trust, but all the while simply transfuses assets from clients to itself while the investors lie on the table etherized by the Wall Street doubletalk.

It was said of Hollywood (by radio comic Ed Gardner) "Scratch away the phony tinsel, and you will find the real tinsel." The same might be said of Wall Street. The first five feet of junk mail (Ten Stocks that are set to Pop Now!!!) may not be to your taste, but the next five feet absolutely will have something that will appeal to you, because your tastes and preferences have been carefully researched. Would you be interested in knowing the name of the investment advisor who had the top track record among the thousands of advisors at Charles Schwab for the past 3, 5, and 10 years? What if I could get you into Bridgewater Associates, the world's biggest hedge fund—up 20 percent in 2011? Unfortunately for you, you might be interested. Your doom is sealed.

It pains me to say this, but you are complicit. You want to believe that the handsome, confident guy with the Patek Philippe watch really is wired in at the highest levels and will take good care of you. You don't want to go to the trouble of understanding what's happening with your money except superficially ("China." "Apple." etc.) You don't want to take a hard look at the numbers to see how he (and by "he" I mean "you") is doing. It is easier to live in denial. Wall Street is counting on it.

THE "FRONT OF THE ENVELOPE" TEST

You've heard of a "back of the envelope" calculation. Here is a quick "front of the envelope" test to determine how you are doing.

Look at the front of the envelope that your monthly or quarterly statements come in. Check the return mailing address in the upper left-hand corner. Does it say one of the following (in no particular order)?

- Vanguard
- Fidelity
- Schwab
- TD Ameritrade
- TIAA-CREF
- T. Rowe Price
- FolioInvesting

If it does not say one of these, you are probably in trouble. Exception: if you buy a fund directly from a mutual fund company, that may be all right, depending on the fund. If the envelope bears the name of a discount brokerage (E*Trade, Options Express, etc.) you may be all right, again depending on what's inside. If the statement is from your 401k plan, you probably are in trouble, but there's little you can do about it at this point.

I hasten to add that even if you are getting your statements from one of these companies, that doesn't mean you are in the clear. This is only a first cut.

How can I make such a blanket prophecy? Because if your statement is from a name-brand Wall Street firm, I can surmise that you are ensnared in one of their Venus flytraps. You were anesthetized by the sticky sweet promise of money while the pod closed around you, and now your fortune is slowly being digested for their benefit. That's how the game is played.

Beware anything that appeals to your sense of entitlement or superiority. Snobs are their easiest victims. If the offer comes in a large envelope embossed in gold lettering, incinerate immediately. If the offices smell like a Ferragamo store, leave. If Warren Buffett doesn't need a swank office, why do these guys? Anything that smacks of exclusivity that suggests that because of your supposed high net worth, they are going to put you in an exclusive club—run!

Otherwise, you will get the special treatment. I once had an investment account held captive by a well-known and prestigious private bank. Jump up and down though I might, I could never get an accounting of their investment performance. Every time I called them on the phone, I had the feeling I was talking to an idiot. I did notice that they seemed to be making money off of me every way imaginable—account management fees, steep commissions, peddling me into securities where they made a market, dealing me individual bonds from their own inventory, putting me into their own mutual funds that all had high internal expense ratios (including index funds charging between one and two percent in annual fees), even charging high fees on cash management. The letterhead said private bank, but in reality it was a glue factory.

After this fiasco was unwound, I described my ordeal to a client. I told him, "Even though the account was supposed to be invested 60 percent in stocks and 40 percent in bonds, I calculated that it had the same volatility as if it were invested 100 percent in the stocks. But the returns, meanwhile, were..."

He interrupted, "I can finish your sentence."

"What?"

"You got the returns of investing in T-bills."

My jaw dropped. "How did you know?" I asked.

"The same thing happens to everyone," he replied.

TRAPS, SNARES, AND DELUSIONS

Fortunately, we know a great deal about what does not work in investing. Before we go into some of the more sensible approaches, we need to clear away some of the traps, snares, and delusions that await the unwary. We are not going to argue these points, because they have been bludgeoned to death elsewhere, but we will list them as a public service. No matter how many times a stake is driven through their heart, they rise from the dead to menace anew, because a number of people have an enormous financial stake in perpetuating them. If these ideas are unfamiliar to you, I refer you to the books by John Bogle or Burton Malkiel.

■ *Smart, well-informed, hard-working, well-connected Wall Street experts beat the market.*

No, they don't. After the fees they charge, they add negative utility. This has been known since the mid-1960s.

■ *Hot managers are hot for a reason, and past performance predicts future performance.*

Hot managers are hot for a while and then (after they're famous enough for you to have heard of them) they go to room temperature. Exception to this rule: the poor performance of the worst managers does persist, usually due to their high internal expense ratios. Bon apetit.

■ *Macroeconomic forecasts have value.*

Astonishingly, many otherwise intelligent people believe that when it comes to the economy, other people—namely, economists—can see into the future. No, Virginia, people cannot see into the future. We would like for them to be able to see into the future, and certainly they would like us to have faith in their ability to see into the future. However, no one can see into the future.

■ *Paying close attention to the financial media is shrewd.*

As entertaining as the financial media are, they exist only as a byproduct of the need to sell financial products. They are like the cartoons in a supermarket pennysaver. Their function is to plate up the "investotainment" that gets you excited about the coupons inside (financial products and services) and get you trading.

■ *Technical analysis "charting" is a way to predict the movements in stock prices.*

Charting is bogus. Graham and Dodd ridiculed it back in 1934, but in investing, bad ideas live forever. Today brokerage firms are happy to give you free charting software so you can automate trading and even trade in foreign markets while you sleep.

When Fischer Black arrived at Goldman Sachs in the 1980s, he confiscated every book he found on technical analysis on the trading floor. That's interesting, don't you think? Wall Street forbids its own employees from using technical analysis, but they encourage you to use it.

■ *Doing solid fundamental analysis is the way to pick market-beating stocks.*

If possible, there is even less validity to this technique than there is to charting. It seems like it should work, but it doesn't. Maybe it did at one time, but it doesn't any more. Financial economist Jack Treynor developed a useful rule of thumb here. Whenever he had an idea for an investment, he would talk it over with his friends. If they liked it and thought it made sense, he immediately dropped it, since he knew this meant his rationale was already in the price.

■ *Gurus, experts, newsletters, five star stocks and funds—yeah, baby!!*

It makes perfect sense that a genius about money who discovered a way to beat the market—a secret worth billions of dollars if it existed—would choose instead to monetize his insight by selling it to chumps like you and me for $299 a year. No, none of these approaches have any value. Newsletters and stock forecasts were comprehensively researched as early as 1933 and proven worthless.

Why doesn't all this stuff work? What is spoiling this exciting party that Wall Street wants you to believe is out there?

PORTFOLIO THEORY 101

We have already seen how Lord Keynes and Graham & Dodd distinguished between investment and speculation, and used security analysis to do bottom-up stockpicking. University of Chicago's Harry Markowitz turned this on its head in 1952 with the publication of "Portfolio Selection" in the *Journal of Finance*. Markowitz argued that stock selection should be done from the top-down. No security could be judged in isolation; it was the whole portfolio that mattered, and a given security could only be measured by its contribution to the whole pie.

The gimmick was that combining many securities gave investors the average of their returns, but less than the average of their separate risks. Since some prices would be up when others were down, the more diversified the portfolio, the more the zigs and zags cancelled each other out. The goal was to get the highest return for the least amount of risk (now defined as portfolio volatility). Portfolios that delivered this were *efficient*. The key to maximizing your risk-adjusted return was to lower risk by maximizing *diversification*: combining as many different kinds of assets as feasible in the portfolio. Diversification was a free lunch, since it cost nothing to achieve. This was better living through the application of mathematics to portfolio construction, and Modern Portfolio Theory came ashore like Venus on a clamshell. Markowitz eventually won a Nobel Prize for his insight.

The next step occurred in 1958 when Yale's James Tobin (Ben's friend and teacher) figured out that, while many portfolios might be relatively efficient, there was indeed one portfolio that was super-efficient, that could not be improved upon by further diversification. It sat on a knife edge where any change one way or the other would cause it to deliver less returns for more risk. Therefore, this was the only portfolio that any rational investor would want to own. The only variable would be how much cash (the risk-free asset) people would hold alongside it. Conservative investors would have a large allocation to cash and a small allocation to the risky super-efficient portfolio; aggressive investors would do the opposite. Tobin wrote this up as "Liquidity Preference as Behavior toward Risk," published it in the *Review of Economic Studies*, and collected a Nobel Prize for this (and other) insights.

The next breakthrough came in 1964, when William Sharpe proved that Tobin's super-efficient portfolio was none other than the "market" portfolio, that is, the portfolio of all risky assets weighted by their price in the market. Sharpe published his paper, "Capital Asset Prices: A Theory of Market Equilibrium under Conditions of Risk" in the *Journal of Finance*, and was awarded a Nobel Prize (along with Markowitz and Merton Miller). This gave rise to the *Capital Asset Pricing Model*. To give credit where it is due, it was understood first by Jack Treynor in 1961.

Instead of having to measure the estimated returns, standard deviations, and correlations among every security in the market a la Markowitz (no small feat in the Stone Age before cheap computing power), the Capital Asset Pricing Model dictated that every security should be priced by how much it varies with the market as a whole. This price contained two components: one part that was integral to the market (its beta), and another part containing anything idiosyncratic beyond that (its alpha). High beta stocks would be more volatile and responsive to market movements than low beta stocks. They would return more, but they would be more risky. There was no free lunch, because higher returns came at the price of higher volatility. The alpha part, which might be positive or negative, represented the risk that could not be diversified by owning the whole market. It was to be avoided since investors were not compensated for assuming it. The riskless asset, cash, earned only the interest rate.

Now they were really frugging! The Center for Research in Securities Prices (CRSP) database was laboriously assembled (400,000 punch cards, 33 reels of magnetic tape, 22,000 pages of printout) on a UNIVAC at the University of Chicago. For the first time, researchers could analyze stock market history empirically, going back to 1926. Everyone was astonished to learn that an unmanaged index of the whole stock market yielded average historical returns of 9 percent per year (Fisher and Lorie, 1964). That should have been the death knell for stockbrokers right there. At the same time, research into the performance of pension funds and mutual funds indicated that their historical performance was no better than that of a random selection of stocks. Theory and practice combined to tell investors they could do better by cutting out the middleman and owning the whole market.

Then, at MIT, Paul Samuelson concluded that future stock prices were unpredictable and followed a "random walk." His paper, "Proof that Properly Anticipated Prices Fluctuate Randomly," was published in the *Industrial Management Review* in 1965; Samuelson collected his Nobel Prize in 1970 for raising the game in economic science. Finally, Eugene Fama coined the *efficient markets hypotheses* in 1966. His research showed that markets quickly assimilate all available information into stock prices. Investors cannot beat the market either by studying trends or performing fundamental security analysis. If there were any information of value to be had from either of these activities, it was already assimilated in the price of the stock. The only reason the price would change was because of news, which by definition was new information.

This was not to say that the current price of a stock is the stock's true intrinsic value, that the price today is the "right" price or a "good" estimate. It is only to say that today's price is equally likely to be high or low, and that no better estimate exists. This insight goes straight back to Louis Bachelier's 1900 doctoral dissertation, the first work of modern quantitative finance. The so-called "true value" is unknowable until after the fact. Otherwise, it would already be incorporated in the price. The market's estimate changes minute by minute as participants with opinions commit using their wallets. A high price yesterday followed by a low price today does not mean that the high price was wrong; it only means that today we have new information, a new consensus. The market is restlessly and relentlessly involved in a quest for price discovery. By 1998 Samuelson concluded with the dictum that the stock market was "micro efficient" (pricing individual stocks) but "macro inefficient" (pricing the market as a whole). Nevertheless, no better measure is available than the market price today.

EFFICIENT MONSTER THEORY

This is all ye know on earth, and all ye need to know: the market rapidly digests all available information and translates it into the price of stocks. While there are various formulations of efficient market theory—a "weak" form, a "semi-strong" form, and a "strong" form—insofar as it affects you, Mr. Affluent Investor, it means give up picking stocks and find another hobby. Your choice is stark: you can spend a lot of time and money on investing with the likely result that you will underperform the market averages, or you can invest passively (which is also economically and tax-efficient) and harpoon better returns than four-fifths of investors per asset class that you invest in. The more asset classes you employ, the more indexing improves your overall odds.

The briefest argument for passive investing may be put thus: there are two groups of investors, active and passive investors. They both own the entire market. The passive investors get the returns of the market less their slight expenses. Active investors try to beat the market, but this is a zero-sum game with winners and losers. Everyone wants to be in the winner's circle, but there are two big problems. One is that winners cannot be identified reliably in advance. The second is that they are expensive. When you add up the returns minus the expenses of the active camp, the passive investor comes out ahead about four-fifths of the time.

Every penny-a-liner who scribbles for the Sunday supplement likes to pen one column per quarter claiming that the efficient market theory is deader than disco, but this is poppycock. The loudest critics of efficient market theory—from Warren Buffett to Robert Shiller to behavioral economists like Richard Thaler—all recommend that we invest the same way that efficient market theory does: passively, by buying a market index fund.

Marshall McLuhan said that the wheel is an extension of the foot and clothing is an extension of the skin. Electric technology is an extension of the central nervous system. With the launch of Telstar in 1962, planet Earth became the content of its own reality TV show. Electric technology has taken the efficient market theory and boosted it by a million volts into a monster. People in London used to get information on the Paris stock market by carrier pigeon. Information today travels everywhere at the speed of light, and markets that used to be merely efficient are now electric. Input is processed into prices by high-speed computers. The efficient monster relentlessly devours information, stomps on Tokyo, and breathes fire onto the active investor, turning him into a burnt match. You can't fight it, not even with an atom bomb. The best you can do is to harness its energy in your portfolio and put the efficient monster in your corner. Let someone else try to slay it. When you fight the invincible foe, you will lose.

THE MING PORTFOLIO

In *Flash Gordon*, Emperor Ming the merciless from the planet Mongo was intent on destroying Earth with his evil death ray. This is shortsighted on Ming's part. He would have been much better off diversifying his Mongo-centric portfolio by investing on Earth, Hoovering up the money year after year for his greater glory. But how should he make this investment?

Looking at our planet through his telescope across space, the regional biases earthlings cling to would simply disappear. Since Ming was from a scientifically advanced civilization, he would be familiar with efficient market theory. He would say to his minions, let me simply index the whole planet.

That is, Ming would want to buy a little of everything: stocks, bonds, commodities, real estate, art, etc. He would want to buy them in the same proportion as they existed in the markets here on Earth. Ming would seek to buy Professor Sharpe's market portfolio: the portfolio of all risky assets.

Right away Ming is in a pickle. There is no way to do this. Financial markets don't exist for all assets. He would have to confine himself to purchasing a first approximation of the market portfolio, which would be the *investable* market portfolio consisting of assets for which there are functioning markets. Furthermore, because he does not want to be saddled with managing millions of unwieldy individual positions, he will look to those places where earthlings have already indexed everything to make accessing the marketwide exposure easy for someone living on Mongo.

Piloting his stratosled to the headquarters of powerball indexers Vanguard at Valley Forge, PA, Ming would ask for their one fund that indexed everything on Earth—the global market portfolio. And Vanguard would explain to him that no such fund exists.

This alone might cause Ming to turn his death ray back on. "What?!?" he would scream. "You (by which he would mean: you mutual fund companies) have thousands of index funds and mutual funds for every possible occasion, but you do not offer the one fund that your own (primitive, by our standards) investment theory says everyone should own: the global market portfolio?" With this, the committee at Vanguard would look at their shoes, stare out the window, and shuffle around uncomfortably, but no, they would have to admit, they did not.

Fortunately for Ming, Niels Bekkers wrote his Master's thesis on this topic and published it in the *Journal of Wealth Management* in 2009 with co-authors Ronald Doeswijk and Trevin Lam as "Strategic Asset Allocation: Determining the Optimal Portfolio with Ten Asset Classes." The omniscient James Picerno (*Dynamic Asset Allocation*) called my attention to it, and I caught up with co-author Doeswijk in 2011to get his latest thinking on the topic before going to press. I present it in Figure 5.1.

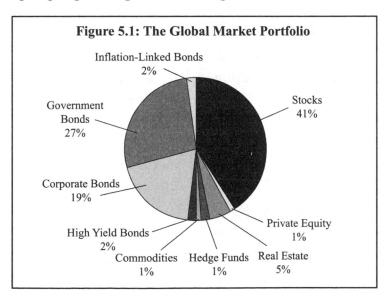

Figure 5.1: The Global Market Portfolio

This pie is only a first step. Now that we've identified what the portfolio looks like, we need to find funds that index each of these categories. Table 5.1 shows one interpretation of the global mosaic captured by exchange-traded funds.

Table 5.1: The Investable Global Market Portfolio		
Asset Class	Ticker	Allocation
Total World Stock Market Index	VT	40.4%
Private Equity	PSP	0.9%
Real Estate	RWO	5.5%
Hedge Funds	QAI	2.5%
Commodities	DJP	0.7%
High Yield Bonds	JNK	1.8%
U.S. Bonds	BND	25.1%
Foreign Bonds	BWX	15%
Emerging Market Bonds	EMB	6%
TIPS	TIP	2.1%

Let's pause for a moment here and behold what is before us. Prometheus has brought us fire from the heavens. This is the apotheosis of modern portfolio theory.

James Picerno periodically visits this evolving topic in his blog (www.thecapitalspectator.com) and I commend it to you. He uses it as the all-purpose benchmark of everything, reports its returns, and periodically discusses which funds to choose for each asset class.

This is the river formed by the confluence of all investments, the Ganges into which every investor dips his cup. The portfolio should be further personalized in two ways. First, we would have to decide how much of the non-risky asset—cash—we should hold alongside it. If we are conservative, we would hold more cash; if aggressive, we would hold less. If we were very aggressive, we could borrow money to buy even more of it.

Second, we would customize it to our personal risk profile. Imagine that you had no skills, no house, no nothing. All you owned was the global market portfolio. So far, so good. Then, you sell some of it to buy a house in East Egg. Portfolio-wise, this is a bad idea: the global portfolio is the ideal investment, and now you have skewed it by making a large, localized, real estate investment. Then you say, why don't I sell some more and go to school and get a medical degree? From an investment point of view, this creates another problem: you have made a particular overinvestment in one market segment and thrown the whole portfolio off kilter. We want the combination of us + the global market portfolio to mirror the global market instead of distorting it. Ideally, we would differ from it only in ways that are market-neutral: adding or subtracting cash to manage our risk.

The impersonal global market portfolio stands at the opposite end of the spectrum from the particularities of our lives. The trick is to marry the two. If our lives give us too much exposure to certain factors, we would change our allocations to everything else so that it completed and counterbalanced us. This does not mean changing the global market portfolio so much as restoring the lost chord: removing the dissonance introduced by our personal over- and under-exposures to various risk factors. This can never be done completely, but taking steps in this direction should be helpful. The point is to diversify our personal risk. Attaining the global portfolio might be seen as the theoretical optimum limit, but there are many useful approximations of this that are attainable.

The global market portfolio would rarely, if ever, require re-balancing. Why not? Because any greater or lesser share of the constituent assets that occurs as a result of price changes simply reflects a change in the underlying global market itself. It's still the global market portfolio. Once captured, the global market portfolio requires no tinkering or fussing. A company like FolioInvesting.com will let you set the initial allocation to these ETFs and will maintain that division even as you add or withdraw cash along the way. This is desirable, because every time you have to change your portfolio, you open a big can of problems. Portfolios that require constant tending invite a lot of mischief and usually prove to be more trouble than they are worth.

PLATO'S RETREAT FOR INVESTORS

In Plato's *Republic* (380 BC), a man finds himself a prisoner of the financial services industry. Chained in a cave, he and his fellow prisoners can only see the back wall. Behind him, the guards dangle various objects in front of a fire, and the prisoners all assume that the shadows flickering across the wall are in fact the real objects, since this is the only reality they have ever known. Some of the prisoners—analysts—give prizes to each other for who can guess how the shadows will move next. They are hypnotized into thinking this kooky world of illusion is real. Yes, Plato has anticipated CNBC.

Our hero breaks free. He turns around and sees the giant manipulation being staged, and escapes to the world of sunlight above. Finally, he looks upon the sun itself, in all its blinding glory. What does he see? Why, he sees Figure 5.1—the global market portfolio—shining like the star of truth.

Then he thinks about the poor prisoners still down in the cave and decides to liberate them. But the path back down is rocky, and he has been temporarily blinded by his vision of the sun. He finds no easy way to convey to them the beauty he has seen—the Platonic form of the perfect portfolio. His old friends are still being manipulated by the guards and think he's gone insane, since now he can no longer even see the shadows dancing on the back wall. They schedule tee times that they know will be inconvenient for him. This is the plight of the globally indexed investor—to be shunned by his deluded stockpicking friends.

ISSUES WITH THE GLOBAL MARKET PORTFOLIO

Our estimates of the initial allocations to the various asset classes are certainly mistaken to some extent. Our portfolio also will be sensitive to tracking errors between the indexes and the universe that the indexes represent, and over time these errors will compound. While this is small beer in the order of problems plaguing investors still chained in the cave, they are worth mentioning. Every few years, check if there have been any updates and rebalance accordingly. Better index funds might come along to distill the portfolio.

In practice, even if you are resolutely determined to set this up, you are likely to have accounts that don't neatly fit into your plans—your 401k, to begin with, where you will have a limited menu of options, and where you will be adding to it periodically with new contributions that distort your effort to keep the overall allocation constant.

Another thing to consider: different accounts tax different asset classes differently. If you are keeping lots of taxable bonds in taxable accounts, this may not be tax-efficient. The global market portfolio is not tax optimized unless its component assets are apportioned into the appropriate investment accounts.

There is something else that may bug you about the global market. It is, well, global. The U.S. only represents about 33 percent of the market capitalization of global equities, and our wedge of the pie has been shrinking over time. These aren't like the good old days when we were rich and everyone else lived in poverty. Now there are a lot of nouveau riche countries around. Academics call a reluctance to invest in global markets on a capitalization-weighted basis the *home'bias*. They consider it an error to be overcome. Yet most Americans are happy to have a measure of home team bias in their portfolios. The home team has done pretty well over the years, and it did especially well relative to the rest of the league of nations during the recent crisis. However, there can be periods of a decade or more when the U.S. lags behind the rest of the world (1999–2009 for a recent illustration). Putting all your money in the leading hot country isn't a good idea, even if you live there, as investors in Japan learned when they invested in 1989 and found their stocks still down 82 percent twenty years later. You want to be globally diversified. The diversified investor is always in the position of wishing he weren't. He wishes he had more of whatever has done well lately and less of whatever hasn't. He is like a married man watching a blonde walk by on the sidewalk. Since he knows this isn't doable, he accepts the returns he gets with philosophic resignation.

A SECOND APPROXIMATION

If the global market portfolio is a beautiful first approximation to the super-efficient market portfolio, but with contingent difficulties not easily resolved in your case, is there a substitute? Maybe you can do something simpler that would be good enough for home use.

The global portfolio is roughly half stocks and half bonds. We could do this with three mutual funds: a total U.S. Stock Market Fund, a total International Stock Market Fund, and a total U.S. Bond Market fund. Let's bake these into a pie (see Figure 5.2).

The advantage here is that the portfolio is very simple and you are even likely to find some of these fund selections inside your 401k. You could park the bonds in your tax qualified account and the stocks in your taxable account. It can be rebalanced once a year. Beyond that, it should command a bare minimum of your attention and free your time for more productive uses, like your work or your family. The virtues of cheap, simple, and easy cannot be overstated when it comes to investing.

The capital asset pricing model assumes there is the super-efficient portfolio of everything and then the riskless asset (cash), with people holding more cash if they are more conservative, or borrowing to lever the global market portfolio if they are aggressive. In practice, people tend to hold enough cash for their comfort level (say, in their emergency fund), and then they vary the bond allocation to control how risky the portfolio is. A high risk portfolio has a low bond allocation, because bonds are (usually) safer than stocks. A low risk portfolio has a high bond allocation for the same reason. If you are young, you might eliminate bonds entirely and be all in equities. If you are in your sixties, you might raise the bond piece to 55 or 60 percent, following the guidelines we proposed earlier.

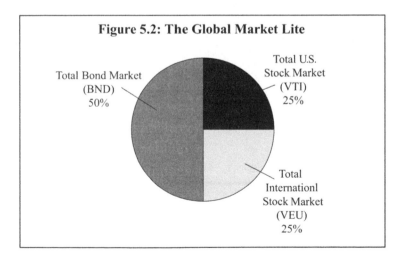

Figure 5.2: The Global Market Lite

Total Bond Market
(BND)
50%

Total U.S.
Stock Market
(VTI)
25%

Total
Internationl
Stock Market
(VEU)
25%

As of this writing, with yields on 10-year treasuries at 1.8 percent, it is an open question how safe the bond market really is. It looks like prices (the inverse of yields) have a long way to fall but not very far to go up, short of a serious deflation. Until the Federal Reserve is done artificially suppressing interest rates, it might be safer to hug the shorter-end of the yield curve.

I urge you to skip the next chapter. Please do not read it. It addresses the terrible question, "Can you do better?"

Chapter Six: Beyond the Valley of the Market Portfolio

Can you do better? You make the call.

The database of securities prices has been sedulously mined by researchers looking for an investment edge. Here are some strategies that have outpaced the market over the historical record.

VALUE STOCKS

In 1977 Sanjoy Basu published "Investment Performance of Common Stocks in Relation to their Price-Earnings Ratios" in the *Journal of Finance*. Basu found that stocks of companies priced at a low multiple of their earnings had about 6 percent better annual returns than those sold at a high price relative to their earnings. This finding was confirmed in later studies using various measures of value, such as price-to dividends and price-to-book value, all of which correlate highly with each other. Basu speculated that growth stocks, by contrast, contained exaggerated investor expectations that tended to disappoint.

Figure 6.1 shows the hypothetical growth of $1 invested in value stocks vs. the S&P 500 from 1927–2011 (before all frictional expenses), courtesy of Ken French's data library. Thank you, Prof.

French! This is as good a place as any to mention that the impressive results you see here would have been unattainable, due to commissions, bid-ask spreads, illiquidity, etc. I present the data not to get you hopped up about hitting some astronomical dollar figure, but to exhibit the historical outperformance of the strategy.

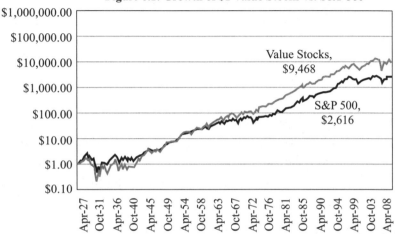

Figure 6.1: Growth of $1 Value Stocks vs. S&P 500

Figure 6.1 makes it look like investing in value stocks is a no-brainer. This exaggerates the ease with which value investors have prospered. What you have is a small difference year-to-year that compounds to a big difference over time. And that's not all: notice that value stocks performed much worse throughout the Great Depression. Do you imagine that it would have been easy sticking by your guns when your stocks were getting pounded far harder than everyone else's? Or, for that matter, in 1999, when value stocks underperformed the teched-up S&P 500 index by 22 percentage points? If you think you have the fortitude to stay the course with an investment agenda in the face of predicaments like those, my guess is that you don't know yourself very well.

DIVIDEND STOCKS

High dividend stocks have outperformed the market going back to 1926. You can buy a worldwide sampling of dividend stocks using three ETFs: Vanguard High Dividend Yield Index (ticker: VYM), the SPDR International Dividend fund (ticker: DWX), and the WisdomTree Emerging Markets Equity Income Fund (ticker: DEM). However, I don't recommend it. Dividend stocks are a subset of value stocks. A high dividend yield is just another value measure like price/earnings or book-to-market ratio. If you are already going the value route, buying high dividend stocks doesn't add anything to the mix, and it may be less effective than some of the more comprehensive measures. If you love dividend stocks, stay tuned. I will have a lot more to say about their role in the next chapter.

SMALL COMPANIES

The evidence that stocks of small companies perform better than the stocks of large companies was first published by University of Chicago Ph.D. Rolf Banz in a 1981 article for the *Journal of Financial Economics*. Banz's abstract gives an excellent summary.

It is found that smaller firms have had higher risk adjusted returns, on average, than larger firms. This "size effect" has been in existence for at least forty years and is evidence that the capital asset pricing model is misspecified. The size effect is not linear in the market value; the main effect occurs for very small firms while there is little difference in return between average sized and large firms. It is not known whether size per se is responsible for the effect or whether size is just a proxy for one or more true unknown factors correlated with size.

We now know this effect has been in existence at least since 1926, and it is found internationally as well. In 1992, when Chicago economists Gene Fama and Ken French published "The Cross-Section of Expected Stock Returns" in the *Journal of Finance*, these findings were codified in the *3-factor model*. CAPM was thrown under the bus. Investment returns are explained by (1) exposure to the stock market (vs. riskless T-bills), (2) exposure to Banz's size factor (small companies have higher returns), and (3) exposure to Basu's value factor (noted above).

This paper spelled curtains for active portfolio management. Any investor's returns were empirically explainable not by elusive stockpicking genius, but by exposure to these three factors. Once you crunch the entire database of mutual funds through this machine there's not much left unexplained, although active management continues because it is so lucrative for the industry.

Figure 6.2 shows the returns of $1 invested small company stocks vs. those in the S&P 500 index since 1927, again courtesy of Ken French's data library.

There is no way to predict which small companies are going to deliver. A few will go on to become the next Google. Others will

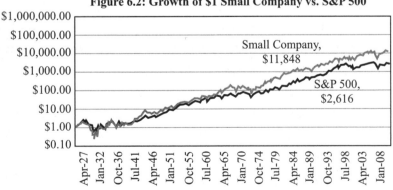

Figure 6.2: Growth of $1 Small Company vs. S&P 500

go out of business. This means you need to diversify by buying a basket of these companies. They are going to be more volatile than bigger, more established companies. That is the part of the extra risk implicit in this bet.

To remind: the returns to these companies may be overstated. There is the issue of survivorship bias: those that have gone on to be delisted from the stock exchange have not always been adequately accounted for in the research. Because these smaller companies can trade infrequently, there are also the factors of stale pricing and illiquidity to contend with. Investors demand compensation for keeping their money tied up, and a large part of the small company premium may amount to a return for their relative illiquidity. Some academics think the small company premium is just a back door to the value premium, to the extent that low price equals value equals a small firm market capitalization.

The small cap effect doesn't happen all the time. You can't go to your ATM and collect the premium every month. It happens in spurts. There can be periods of many years when there is no small cap premium in evidence. Dimensional Funds, the mutual fund company that was started by the University of Chicago academics to cash in on these risk factors, opened their microcap fund as their premiere offering at the end of 1981, and—with timing that perfectly reflects how investing works in the real world—the small cap effect immediately went into hiding. As the years went by, people openly speculated that the effect had vanished and that Dimensional was chasing a rainbow. Then it reappeared. Imagine that you were one of the initial investors. You would have been richly rewarded for your patience, but you would have had to persevere for years when small caps were out of favor to get the prize out of this crackerjack box.

SMALL VALUE STOCKS

If small is beautiful, and value beats growth, then why not have the best of both worlds: small value stocks? Figure 6.3 shows the performance of small value stocks from 1927–present, courtesy of Ken French's data library. Their performance is spectacularly better than either that of the S&P 500 or of a portfolio made up 50/50 of small cap stocks and large value stocks.

Again, this is not to say that these returns were capturable, or that it is easy to follow this discipline in practice. Depending on when you jump on the small/value bandwagon you might be in for ten or more years of rough road before you realize any outperformance. If that happens to you, it is likely that you will be seduced by some other idea along the way.

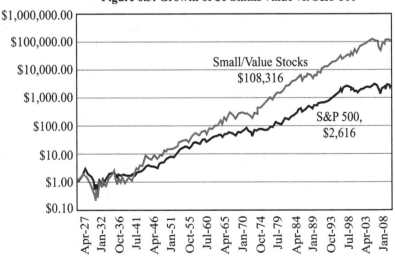

Figure 6.3: Growth of $1 Small/Value vs. S&P 500

MOMENTUM

Momentum refers to the tendency of stocks that have performed well (or poorly) lately to continue to perform well (or poorly). Traders have known this forever. Academics came late to the party but quantified the effect when they arrived. Pioneers include Jegadeesh and Titman ("Returns to Buying Winners and Selling Losers," 1993) and Cliff Asness's University of Chicago doctoral dissertation ("Variables that Explain Stock Returns," 1994). By now it is a robust, widely recognized investment style that is understood to operate across financial markets. In 1997, Mark Carhart combined it with Fama & French's 3-Factor model to create (drum roll) the 4-factor model: market, size, value, and momentum. This is theory evolving: Asness and Carhart were both students of Fama's at Chicago. Further models were subsequently developed, including Ross's Arbitrage Pricing Theory and Merton's Intertemporal Capital Asset Pricing Model, but they need not concern us here.

The momentum strategy is to buy the stocks that have done the best over the medium term (say, the past two months to two years). Cliff Asness describes the drill. A colleague would show him a trade, and he would ask, "Are we buying more of Company X simply because the price is higher than last month?" His colleague would than look at him solemnly and say, "Yes, we are." And Asness would say, "Fine, just checking." This is not something you can do at home, because trading costs would quickly erode your profits, and managing the portfolio would be extremely time-consuming even if trading were free.

Figure 6.4 shows the performance of momentum stocks vs. the S&P 500 from 1927–present, courtesy of Ken French. Again, these accrue in a frictionless Eden where there are no taxes, commissions, or market impact costs. But they are beguiling.

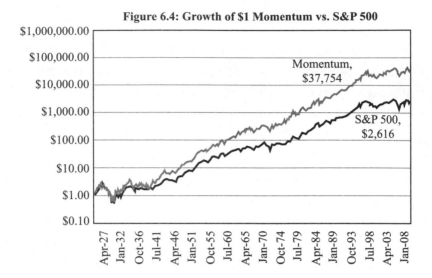

Figure 6.4: Growth of $1 Momentum vs. S&P 500

Regrettably, the momentum anomaly is not so easy to cash in as the other ones noted here. While there are hundreds of small cap and value funds, retail investors have few options in the momentum space. This should change as investors awaken to the opportunity. Another feature of momentum investing is that it has only a modest correlation with small/value stocks, and can pick up the slack when small/value investing is out of favor (and vice versa). This makes them a good team inside a portfolio. The idea is that value investing is the long-term "buy low" strategy, and momentum is the short-term trading position around it.

LOW-BETA STOCKS

Low-beta stocks are those that have a low correlation to the stock market as a whole. They are similar, but not identical, to low volatility stocks, which are stocks whose prices do not jump around very much. Most low beta stocks are low volatility stocks and vice versa. These are often companies found within the utility, consumer staple, and health care sectors, companies where there is a constant, inelastic demand for their goods and services no matter how the larger economy is faring.

The low beta anomaly was the first to be discovered of all of the ones discussed here, but the last to be made available to retail investors. It is also the least familiar, so I will devote the most time to explaining it. I am indebted to Peter Bernstein, Perry Mehrling, Kate Ancell, Wayne Wagner, and Myron Scholes for helping me pull the story together.

In the 1960s, Wells Fargo spent millions of dollars on computers, but was using them to perform prosaic tasks like mailing customer statements. They wondered if computers might be able to do something more interesting, like pick stocks. This was at a time when the largest computer available to Wells in San Francisco —the IBM 7094—was as big as a room, cost $500 an hour to use, was controlled by punch cards, and had less processing power and memory than an iPhone.

To answer this question, Wells Fargo's Bill McQuown assembled the Legion of Super-Heroes of quantitative finance, consulting with Harry Markowitz, Bill Sharpe, Gene Fama, Merton Miller, Lawrence Fisher, Mike Jensen, Jim Lorie, David Booth, Oldrich Vasicek, Bill Fouse, Wayne Wagner, Myron Scholes, and Fischer Black, among others. By 1968, the smart guys in finance had analyzed the performance of pension funds and mutual funds, and knew that active stockpicking was a sham. Contrary to the self-serving mythology, most managers did not beat the S&P 500 index. Their revolutionary recommendation to Wells Fargo was to forget stockpicking, computerized or otherwise, jettison active management (Wells's prestigious "Financial Analysis" department), and buy the market. This simple advice changed the landscape of investing.

Unhappily, there was nothing sexy about just matching the market's returns as a sales proposition. Wells was resolved to beat it. One way would be to buy only high-beta stocks. Another way would be to leverage the market portfolio. Neither would beat the market on a risk-adjusted basis, but the returns would at least be better on the upside. However, Myron Scholes and Fischer Black knew there was a kink in the new capital asset pricing model. Black, Scholes, and Wagner did an investigation ranking stocks by beta and then looking at the long-range returns. They found that stocks tended to have similar returns no matter what their betas were; only their volatilities differed. Low beta stocks delivered something like a market level of return, but for less than a market level of risk.

Black understood that by using leverage, you could gear up the returns of low beta stocks until they had the same volatility as the stock market as a whole. This would give you better-than-market returns for a market level of risk. He and Scholes advised Wells Fargo that this was how to run their flagship Stagecoach fund. The idea was shot down by Wells's Bill Fouse, who was concerned that the low beta portfolio would be underdiversified. The clinically reserved Black stalked out of the meeting.

The Stagecoach fund that finally launched was just a leveraged market index fund. Its edge was the bank's cheap cost of borrowing. However, the Investment Company Institute (the mutual funds' trade association) brought suit to stop banks from launching mutual funds, and invoked the Glass-Steagall Act to squash their competition. Then, the leverage feature kicked it into a hornet's nest of SEC prohibitions, bank regulations, and reticence from lenders. The fund died in 1973.

Meanwhile, back at the University of Chicago, Keith Shwayder—whose family owned Samsonite Luggage —was unhappy with the performance of their company's pension funds. He knew about the work being done at Wells Fargo and suggested that his dad give them $6 million of pension money to manage.

As a result, in 1971 the Samsonite Luggage Pension Fund became the world's first index fund. It was not the capitalization-weighted fund that we know and love today, a la Vanguard. Wells created an *equal-weight fund* using all 1,500 companies listed on the New York Stock Exchange. This fund was a logistic nightmare to operate and expensive to rebalance, given the primitive trading tools of the day. It ran aground during the recession in 1974, and was finally disbanded in 1976 in favor of a market price weighted strategy using the S&P 500 Composite Index. By that time, a few other cap-weighted index funds had appeared. The idea was in the air. John Bogle took it to Vanguard and the rest is history.

The equal-weight index fund did not return until 2003. Wells Fargo did not appreciate how prescient they had been (possibly they still don't). By buying all the stocks on the exchange instead of just the leading stocks, they made the size of the average company in the portfolio smaller, capturing the small company effect. Then, by equal-weighting the companies instead of price-weighting them, they shifted the portfolio away from the more expensive growth stocks and pushed it toward the beaten-down value stocks. By inadvertence, they created the first index fund with a small/value tilt, decades ahead of their time.

The first mutual fund with an explicit low beta mandate was not launched until 2011, over forty years after Black, Jensen, and Scholes proposed it at a Wells Fargo conference in August 1969 at the University of Rochester. This presentation was published in 1972 ("The Capital Asset Pricing Model: Some Empirical Tests") where they announced that "market portfolio excess returns indicated that high-beta securities had significantly negative intercepts and low-beta securities had significantly positive intercepts, contrary to the predictions…." Even twenty years later, when Chicago economists Fama and French published their dispositive data in "The Cross-Section of Expected Stock Returns" in the *Journal of Finance*, little was made of this part of their finding. Meanwhile, as Frazzini has demonstrated, Warren Buffett had already gotten rich faithfully following the method Black *et al.* prescribed: buying low beta companies and using leverage (float) to goose his return. The real mystery is that it was not more widely deployed.

The best explanation goes back to one of the objections that Wells Fargo encountered: leverage aversion. There are many people in the financial marketplace who cannot use leverage. Mutual funds keep about eight percent of their holdings in cash to meet redemptions. They can't lever their portfolios to compensate for this drag, so they buy high beta stocks instead. Pension funds often are precluded from using leverage by their mandates. Individual investors can go on margin, but it is expensive and cumbersome. Finally, money managers who are benchmarked to market indexes have an incentive not to use low-beta stocks, as we will see shortly.

Figure 6.5 shows how low beta/low volatility stocks have performed 1926–2011, courtesy of AQR Capital and Frazzini & Pedersen's white paper, "Betting Against Beta."

This spectacular performance of low beta stocks is largely due to the fact that the low beta stocks double dip into the small company and value stocks. These results would have been unattainable due to the problems with illiquidity, stale pricing, commissions, market impact, bid-ask spreads, and so forth. A more realistic expectation would be for low beta stocks to roughly match the returns of the market over an economic cycle, but to outperform during bear markets and underperform during bull markets. Investors need to live with them through a down draft to see their value and not jettison them when they lag during the good times. Their counter-cyclical behavior makes them especially valuable, because an investment that outperforms when everything else withers is a friend in time of trouble.

These stocks have a low correlation to the market and a low correlation to each other as well. That means a portfolio of low beta stocks has a high degree of internal diversification, which means it offers high risk-adjusted returns (Geoff Considine has proposed this as one mechanism behind their relative outperformance). They beat the market because wins and losses are not symmetrical, and it pays to lose less. If you are down 50 percent, you have to make back 100 percent to break even. But if you only lose 25 percent, you "only" have to make back 33 percent to get to the starting line. A low beta stock fund might be down 25 percent when the market as a whole is down 40 percent.

The funds that have piled into this domain in the aftermath of 2008 employ a variety of strategies: low beta, low volatility, minimum variance, high quality company, low liquidity, and so on. Some try to be sector-neutral, others overweight the leading low beta sectors such as utilities. Fortunately, the strategy is fairly robust

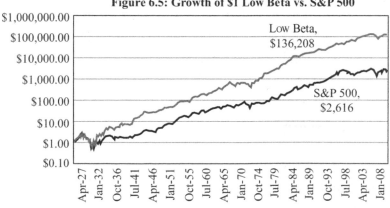

Figure 6.5: Growth of $1 Low Beta vs. S&P 500

with respect to whichever tactic is employed. Readers who want to keep up to date with the latest developments in all things low beta are referred to Eric Falkenstein's entertaining blog (http://falken-blog.blogspot.com/).

THE BENCHMARK PARADOX

Harvard's Howard Baker offers another explanation why people don't own low beta equities: agency problems and tracking error. Agency problems crop up when people doing things on behalf of others have their own agenda that takes precedence. Tracking error is how much a fund deviates from the benchmark that it is measured against. Both create difficulties for low beta investors.

The typical money manager's investment strategy is to hug the index as closely as he can, and then take a little more risk by buying the latest hot stocks so he beats it. This pays off, because on average the market is up two years out of three, and people mostly invest new money during the good times and all they look at is a manager's recent performance: is he beating the index? If so, money flows in. Of course, during bad times, his game collapses—but then so does everyone else's. The money manager hides under his desk until the storm passes. Then, he does it again. This is the business model of the financial services industry.

However, if the money manager were to buy low beta stocks, even though he might beat the benchmark in the long run, his quarter-to-quarter results would be, well, different. There would be many times when he is the cheese who stands alone. This is career death. It means losing clients and failing to attract new ones, precisely when his competitors are advertising their market-clobbering returns. Much as he would enjoy being alone and right, he absolutely cannot afford to be alone and wrong. He follows Keynes precept from the *General Theory*, "Worldly wisdom teaches that it is better for reputation to fail conventionally than to succeed un-conventionally." As Barker points out, the people who are paid to put investors' interests first put their own interests first. The anvil of quarterly performance benchmarking hangs over the entire pro-fession, and encourages advisors to game the system instead of serving the client. The paradoxical result is that the focus on bench-marking ends up costing investors money.

Benchmarking has other hidden costs as well. It means that managers will expend 95 percent of their resources covertly recre-ating the benchmark index—which investors could get with an index fund for pennies—and then add a thin slice of their own spe-cial magic, for good or evil, for which investors will be charged a relative fortune. Managers spend most of their time hiding behind the benchmark fig leaf.

What is an investor to do? Discard benchmarking altogether, and you are adrift. Benchmarks at least protect you from the most incompetent actors.

There are two alternatives. One is to be the benchmark. Index everything by using the market portfolio or one of its variants, as discussed in the last chapter. Thereafter, you don't need to worry about benchmarking because you are the benchmark. Index every asset class where you invest.

The second approach is to invest by strategy, as proposed in this chapter, and dispense with benchmarking your returns, except over long periods. This presumes that you are following a disci-plined, systematic approach within each subcategory and paying reasonable fees.

Your bet is that if the strategy has outperformed the bench-mark index from 1927–present across global markets, it will con-tinue to outperform. Once you have made that call, measuring your performance against the benchmark month-to-month, quarter-to-quarter, or even year-to-year is not going to be revelatory. If anything, it will tempt you to make a dumb decision, i.e., microcap stocks have been lagging for five years, let's dump them and put the money into something that has been outperforming lately instead.

In other words, if you want to outperform the market, you are going to have to follow the Tao of benchmark indifference. Human beings are innately competitive, and it is going to hurt not being up 20 percent that year when all of your friends are up 20 percent. Your ability to eschew envy and not go with the crowd will determine your success in following the strategies outlined here, because no strategy works all the time (if it did, it would be a money machine and not a strategy). During the times when you are wandering in the desert, all you will have to fall back upon is the strategy's underlying economic intuition. If you don't understand what you are doing and why you are doing it, it will be hard not to capitulate at what is almost certainly the wrong time.

WHY DO THESE STRATEGIES WORK?

There is considerable debate about why these findings exist. We have spent some time discussing the scaffolding behind low beta investing. We will now consider them as a piece.

Brainiacs from the University of Chicago—the fastest guns in town—champion belief in efficient markets. This leads them to conclude that outperformance in one area must be counterbalanced by risk, even if that risk is not fully understood. Gunslingers at other universities, trying to bag a few Nobel prizes of their own, posit other explanations: The market is inefficient and irrational, or perhaps these anomalies can be explained by behavioral factors.

These anomalies arose in the context of the capital asset pricing model and efficient market theory. The problem is, the volatility (the usual operational definition of risk) of small company and value stocks is less than the theory would predict. I buttonholed Professor Fama at a conference and asked him about this. He replied that there are risks beyond those captured by standard deviation. He asked me to consider a portfolio of…and here he rattled off the names of six stocks that were in the news because they were in trouble. "Nobody wants a portfolio like that. It feels too risky." Value and size are thereby promoted to "risk factors" for which investors deserve to be compensated. But this still leaves momentum and low beta sticking out, because no one has proposed convincing risk factors for these.

To wonder why value, small company, low beta, and momentum stocks outperform is to ask the question the wrong way. The better question is, why do investors overinvest in speculative growth stocks that so often disappoint? The truth is, investors are fearful creatures who seek comfort buying the famous, glamorous, in-the-news companies that everyone else is also buying in the hope that it will make them rich. As investors crowd into the latest new thing, they end up overpaying for a fantasy of growth. This has a number of sub-components, including:

- Overconfidence (insecurity)

- Overtrading

- Mental laziness

- Hysteria

- Wishful thinking

- Sub-optimal math skills

- Performance chasing

- Lack of knowledge of market history

- Availability bias (what's on CNBC today)

- Contagious magic

- Ego identification (Starbucks, Apple, etc.: I am what I own)

- Social cachet

- Groupthink

- Herding

- Risky Shift

- Plausible deniability in the event of failure

In a world like this, the smart move is not to follow the lemmings off the cliff. This fate is avoided by value, small company, low beta, and momentum strategies. Value, small company, and low beta strategies sidestep the rush, while momentum strategies join in for a while but then mechanically pull out, following a kind of investment "rhythm" method. You can still lose lots of money following these strategies, as they all swim in the same waters that the market does. However, over time, at the margin, they can protect you from some of the long-term disappointment that accrues to speculation.

The consolation of the "risk factor" argument is that these effects can be relied upon to persevere. Our enhanced payout is the prize for enduring the risk. By comparison, psychological explanations seem vaporous. Yet there is also consolation to be had in following a strategy that bets against a deep-seated characteristic of human nature. If these effects have persevered even after their discovery forty years ago, they should still have some shelf life. Notice what little success programs have met with in trying to remake human psychology, from psychoanalysis to the Hitler youth to the new Soviet Man.

Table 6.1 shows some tickers for some funds that try to capture these effects. You can punch them into the investment site Morningstar.com to learn more about them. Note that many people try to combine the small/value effect into one fund. You will need an investment advisor to get into the "advisor" funds, which typically are from Dimensional Fund Advisors or AQR Capital. You can find tax-managed versions of some of these funds as well, although they are not listed here. The retail offerings are almost all exchange-traded funds. In some cases, they may be thinly traded.

Table 6.1: Funds for Factors				
		U.S.	Foreign	Emerging Market
Small Company	Retail	VB	SCZ	DGS
	Advisor	DFSCX	DFISX	DEMSX
Value	Retail	VTV	EFV	DGS
	Advisor	DFLVX	DFIVX	DFEVX
Small/Value	Retail	PRFZ	PDN	PXH
	Advisor	DFSVX	DISVX	DFCEX
Momentum	Retail	BRSMX	N/A	N/A
	Advisor	AMOMX	AIMOX	AIMOX
Low Beta	Retail	SPLV	EFAV	EEMV
	Advisor	AUEIX	ANDIX	AZEIX

Note that there are not many good retail momentum funds available yet; that could change as the ones that have started gather more assets under management (such as HMTM and XMTM).

PORTFOLIO ALLOCATION

How do you integrate these caffeinated strategies into your portfolio? There is no *a priori* solution: good arguments can be made for 0 to 100 percent allocations. The more you tilt away from the market portfolio, the greater your possibility of excess returns, but also the greater your certainty of different returns, which you will love when you trounce the competition, but have you feeling like life's loser during the inevitable periods when they underperform.

How much should you allocate to each? While we already have the envelope with the answer for 1926–present, we do not have the envelope with the answer for the remainder of your investment lifetime. Under conditions of uncertainty, a defensible approach is to divide your money equally among these three strategies, putting 1/3rd in each: small/value, low beta, momentum. This sounds naïve but you would be surprised how often this works. It is a great way to go unless you have a better idea. As these findings have been cross-validated in foreign markets, you will want to apply the model to international equities as well, perhaps parking 60 percent of your equity model in U.S. stocks, and 30 percent in foreign developed markets, and 10 percent in emerging markets (to pick some numbers out of a hat). In the meantime, you should rebalance the portfolio every year or two or whenever the allocation veers away from the model by five percentage points, selling whatever has done well and using the proceeds to bring up the underdogs (or, better, using new cash to rebalance without selling anything).

LIFE STAGE ALLOCATION USING MARKET ANOMALIES

Another way to approach asset allocation with anomalies is to consider it in the context of your life stage. We mentioned in Chapter Three that most young adults, up to age 35, should be 100 percent in equities—or higher, if there were some cheap and easy way to leverage their accounts. Well, there is. They can invest in asset classes whose expected returns are higher than those of the market. That would be the small/value stocks and momentum stocks. This should manifest higher returns without the problems that using leverage entails.

Then, as they grow older, during their peri-retirement years (ages 55–75), they could switch into low beta stocks. This should give them close to a market return with less risk. Parenthetically, I wonder whether some advisors using Dimensional Funds are really serving their clients well by loading them up with volatile small/value stocks during this stage of their lives.

Finally, late in life, if all has gone well, they could shift back into the small/value and momentum approaches.

Your ability to do this would also have to take into account the tax consequences of making these trades, as well as real world obstacles like the limited investment choices inside your 401k plan. But here is one illustration of how the flow could go:

Start by using an equity index fund inside your 401k (a S&P 500 Index fund or similar). Small/value and momentum stocks probably will not be available as options, or if they are, the expense ratios would be prohibitive.

Then, open a taxable account that you fund with small/value and momentum stock funds.

Once you hit 35, let your small/value and momentum stocks ride. Start adding low beta stocks in your taxable account while you gradually sell your stock index fund inside the 401k and replace it with the cheapest generic bond index fund, to bring your overall asset allocation to the desired stock/bond ratio for your age and life-situation.

In midlife, as your salary rises and you are able to save more, build up your low beta position substantially. By retirement, don't sell your small/value and momentum stocks unless there is a low tax opportunity; offset them with bonds in your tax-deferred accounts and low beta stocks elsewhere. If you have changed jobs along the way—which I deem certain—you will also be able to move your old firm's 401k plan to a rollover IRA where you will have better investment choices.

In other words, tailor the allocation to each asset class according to your life stage. As for investing once you hit retirement, well…that gets a chapter all its own.

Chapter Seven: Retire the Warren Buffett Way

To retire like Warren, all you need to do is:

1. Save $46 billion
2. Retire

In the unlikely event that Warren Buffett were to retire, his $46 billion is sufficient to keep him in a doublewide and still leave a little left over for a Caribbean cruise. Is there anything that prospective retirees can learn from Warren's own investment principles?

GET THE JUICE, BRUCE

It is often said that Berkshire Hathaway, Warren's company, has never paid a dividend, but this is false. In 1967, Berkshire Hathaway declared a dividend of ten cents per share. Warren stopped this wretched excess because he had better ideas about how to spend that dime to make more money for his shareholders.

According to the 1958 Nobel-prize winning Modigliani-Merton indifference theorem, it shouldn't matter what a firm's dividend policy is. It shouldn't matter whether a shareholder's return comes from capital appreciation (a price increase of the stock, the result of reinvested earnings, or perhaps animal spirits) or dividends. Other things being equal, you could raise money by selling shares of a company or by pocketing a dividend check. There is no reason to prefer one approach to the other, at least pre-tax.

And yet... in practice, stocks that pay dividends have performed better for investors. Robert Arnott and Cliff Asness, in a 2003 article surveying 130 years of stock market history in the *Financial Analysts Journal*, discovered that corporate profits grew fastest in the decade after high dividend payouts, and were lowest in the years after low dividend payouts—exactly the opposite of what we might expect. This suggests that, unlike Buffett, most CEOs destroy shareholder value through boneheaded acquisitions and fatuous projects. Their empire building causes them to be trumped by companies that pay high dividends. Buffett's famous 1984 letter to shareholders says that unless management creates a dollar of shareholder value for every dollar of retained earnings, the earnings should be distributed as dividends—exactly as his guru Benjamin Graham maintained.

Some people take high dividend stocks as a valid substitute for bonds, especially in a low-yield environment. This overlooks the fact that stocks are generally far more volatile than bonds. However, bonds can be dangerous, too. Retirees need to be alert to dangers from all sides of their fortress. The guiding principle of the bond side of a portfolio should be to stay out of trouble.

There are a number of exchange-traded funds starring high dividend stocks. Table 7.1 gives a cross-section of some current U.S. offerings.

These funds are subdivisions of the value investing strategy we described in the last chapter. They implicitly take a "numbers" approach to diversification. If a portfolio holds 100 stocks, it must be more diversified than one that holds 50 stocks, even if they are all the same kind of stocks. This has the effect of diluting the dividend yield, which was the motive for buying the fund in the first place, in order to give us a more stock market-like level of diversification, which we don't need, while raising the fund's beta, which we don't want. In other words, there are issues with using funds like these.

Can we do better?

While Berkshire Hathaway does not pay dividends, the companies that it buys do. In fact, according to a recent analysis by Frazzini, Kabiller, and Pedersen, "...the secret behind Buffett's success is the fact that he buys safe, high-quality, value stocks." Let me translate. By "safe, high-quality" they mean *profitable, large, low beta, high credit quality companies*. By value, they mean *high dividend* (or at least high earning) companies acquired at good prices. This could be key to paying for your retirement.

Table 7.1: U.S. Dividend ETFs			
Name	**Ticker**	**Expense**	**Yield**
iShares DJ Select Dividend Index	DVY	0.40%	3.56%
SPDR S&P Dividend	SDY	0.35%	3.14%
Vanguard High Dividend Yield	VYM	0.13%	2.97%
PowerShares Dividend Achievers	PEY	0.60%	3.99%
WisdomTree LargeCap Dividend	DLN	0.28%	3.35%
Schwab U.S. Dividend	SCHD	0.07%	2.36%
iShares High Dividend	HDV	0.40%	3.28%

What about taking a shortcut, buying Berkshire Hathaway and selling a few shares every year to pay for your frappuccinos? Many a comfortable retirement has been funded in precisely this manner. Early investors who bought in during Berkshire's period of astronomical capital appreciation found themselves buoyed on a sea of money. Unfortunately, Buffett does not predict this for the next generation. More problematic is the fact that, while Berkshire is a low beta stock (about 0.25 compared to the market), its volatility has been about 1.4× that of the stock market as a whole, due to the 1.6× leverage it uses from the cash "float" from its underlying businesses. Retirees might be more comfortable keeping the low beta/high value part while forgoing the leveraged/higher volatility part.

Diving for Dividends

In *Yes, You Can Supercharge Your Portfolio*, Ben and I suggested that instead of trying to optimize an income portfolio's Sharpe ratio (returns/risk), we would do better to optimize its risk-adjusted yield (yield/risk). This turns out to be a good idea, because dividends and volatility are more predictable than future returns. Once a company establishes the discipline of issuing a regular dividend, it is loath to cut it because of the bad signal that sends to the stock market.

When I do this for clients, I optimize a portfolio with the group of stocks with the highest minimum historical dividend yield with the least amount of risk. But there is a version of this game you can play at home. Here's what I would do if I were trapped on a desert island with only a calendar, a mattress, and a high-speed Internet connection. To survive, I would eat the dates off the calendar and drink water from the springs of the mattress. Then I would log on to the Internet to use the stock screeners at Yahoo, Bing, CNBC, or Morningstar.com. I would screen for stocks that meet the following criteria:

■ Dividend Yield: between 4 and 6 percent

Rationale: If I am going to the trouble of picking individual stocks, I need to be compensated with a greater yield than is available from the prepackaged dividend ETFs. You can look up their yields and use them as a lower limit. I want to get an average yield from the group that is higher than the conventional retiremen drawdown rate of 4 percent, which I can always take from a portfolio on a total returns basis by selling off a piece of it every year to create a synthetic dividend.

There are also going to be lots of stocks yielding more than 6 percent (or, say, 3× whatever the stock market is yielding). I don't want them. I just assume they could be trouble.

■ Historical Dividend Increase: 0% or more

Rationale: While dividend investors often focus on companies that consistently raise their dividends, this is not our concern. We don't care at all about consistent dividend raisers (although we have nothing against them). We are fine with companies that only raise their dividends intermittently. We are looking for consistent dividend payers. We want to filter out companies that have cut their dividends. Our working assumption is that these consistent dividend payers in aggregate will raise their dividends in line with inflation, but how and when they do this we will leave up to management and the dividend gods.

■ Payout Ratio: under 60 percent

Rationale: Some dividend payouts may be unsustainably high. For most of the companies you are interested in, a payout under 60 percent should be sustainable. The payout ratio is like a waist-to-hip ratio that screens out the most untenable dividends. It also will screen out Real Estate Investment Trusts, to be considered later.

■ Market Capitalization: $2 billion or more

Rationale: Big companies are more stable than small companies, and this whole endeavor is about generating a stable income stream. Many institutional investors will automatically screen out companies under $10 billion. We are not concerned about market impact with our individual 100 or 500 share purchases, so we can pick over the slightly smaller companies for any low-hanging fruit the big boys have left behind. But generally speaking, size matters: bigger is better.

■ Price/Earnings: under 20, preferably under 15

Rationale: This is a way to avoid grossly overpaying, and the convention will vary from industry to industry. We are buying a stream of earnings, and if we overpay, it is difficult to extract value from our investment. Graham and Dodd felt buying stocks at a P/E above 20 was speculation and that buyers who did this would be likely to lose money in the long run.

■ Beta: less than 0.50

Rationale: I want a portfolio to covary as little as possible with the stock market. The more insulation I can buy, the better. The lower the beta of the constituent stocks, the higher diversification of the portfolio, since the primary underlying risk factor—market risk—has been minimized. This means I am getting more yield per unit of risk—a portfolio free lunch. Morningstar has every metric on our list except this one, which you will have to get from one of the other online screeners.

■ Standard Deviation: under 25%

Rationale: While stocks may be low beta, they can still be volatile, and that volatility will jerk around the dividend yield. I prefer stocks that are placid, low temperature investments. Morningstar is the only popular screener I have seen that lists the trailing 3-year standard deviation of the stock price.

■ Financial Health Grade: B or better

Rationale: This Morningstar metric covers a number of sins, such as companies with too much leverage or insufficient free cash flow. The idea is to select companies with a margin of safety in an economic downturn.

You can supplement the list with any other criteria that tick your boxes. For example, you might want to mosey over to Moody's and check the credit ratings of your picks, choosing the highest credits.

My next step is to winnow this list. I discard any mutual funds that have passed through the sieve. These will be exchange-traded funds or closed-end funds (more about these in due course). I also expunge any limited partnerships because I do not want the hassle of having to file K-1s with my tax returns. I skip most foreign stocks and ADRs, since all the metrics may not be available for them.

Finally, I would eliminate any companies I didn't like for any reason I pleased. I would never let a checklist shoehorn me into buying anything. The acid test for the value investor is that you shouldn't buy a company unless you would buy it even if no market existed for its shares. As you review each company, it should have a transparent, idiot-proof business model that has been around for decades.

Secret ingredient time: Other things equal, choose the stocks with the lowest betas on the list. These are going to cluster in the utility, consumer staple, and healthcare industries. The goal is to choose around twenty securities, diversifying across industries as much as possible.

This portfolio is tilted heavily toward the "investment" side of the "investment vs. speculation" continuum. These companies are often dismissed as "widows and orphans" stocks—like that's a bad thing? It will look like an underdiversified portfolio, but it is diversified enough to meet our purposes. Even a portfolio of electric utilities can have a surprising amount of diversification, because the demand for electricity is determined primarily by the weather, and a cool summer in New York can be offset by a hot summer in Dallas. The overweighting of health care companies is another good thing. Retirees have sizable out-of-pocket health care costs, and this will help hedge those expenses.

During the recent financial crisis, dividends overall fell (temporarily) by 23 percent. This strategy would not have protected you as much as you would heve liked. Had you gone through this operation before the crash in 2008, there probably would have been financial companies on your list. These companies were lying about their earnings, because they failed to withhold adequate reserves as provision for bad debts. Many of their liabilities deliberately were held as off-balance-sheet transactions, designed to avoid regulatory and accounting scrutiny.

Researchers Kinlaw, Kritzman, and Turkington have come up with an interesting concept called *asset centrality*, which tries to measure an asset class's vulnerability to failure by looking at how central it is to the economy, and notably, how exposed it is to the riskier parts of the financial system. Their data suggest that the utility, consumer staples, health care, industrial, and materials sectors are the best insulated, while the financial, energy, and telecom sectors are especially vulnerable. Although we don't know how this will pan out in the future, a retiree might find it worthwhile to overweight/underweight his dividend stock investments in these sectors, respectively. This would have helped a lot in 2008. If we are faced with an inflationary scenario, financials would be especially vulnerable, since inflation transfers wealth from lenders to borrowers. But oil and gas stocks would do better, because of their ability to quickly reprice in response to market conditions (a fact you may have noticed if you occasionally put gas in your car).

CATS AND DOGS

There are lots of dividend-yielding investments out there, some of them nutty, some of them nice. The rule is, make sure you can see the gumball in the gumball machine before inserting your penny. Here is a fast, opinionated tour.

■ Foreign Dividend Stocks

Love them. I would buy them in an exchange-traded fund. There is the S&P International Dividend SPDR (ticker: DWX, currently yielding 6.2 percent as we go to press). For emerging markets, there is the WisdomTree Emerging Markets Equity Income fund (ticker: DEM, currently yielding 4 percent). No doubt there are other funds that are as good. I would include each of these in my arsenal, even though they are not low beta.

■ Real Estate Investment Trusts

Love them. I would run all the filters above but set the payout ratio screen for under 175% and the beta screen for under 80. If some REITs popped up that looked great, I would add them to the list. If not, I would add two Vanguard exchange-traded REIT funds to my list: tickers VNQ (domestic) and VNQI (international). Their distributions are taxed more heavily than those of dividend stocks. Remember that REITs are leveraged investments and will be hurt in a credit crisis like we had in 2008. However, REITs were also the best performing asset class during the inflation of the 1970s, when stocks and bonds lost half their value. It's worth repeating: inflation is the great enemy of retirees.

■ Closed-End Funds

These funds were initially created to generate sales commissions. After the initial offering, they hover in no-man's-land, generally selling at a discount to the net asset value of their holdings. Most of them are leveraged, and so they offer extremely high yields. I have yet to find one where the high yield was a bargain, considering the elevated risk. You always want to buy them at a substantial discount to NAV; that is your margin of safety. Unless investing in these funds is a specialty of yours, leave them to others.

■ Dividend Capture Funds

The idea here is that the dividend capture fund swoops down like an eagle and snares the fat dividend from a company just as it is released, then holds the stock for 90 days for tax purposes, and sells it. Of course, what the fund gains in dividends it loses in net asset value, plus increased trading costs. In a bull market, the ensuing price appreciation of the stock will boost your returns; in a down market, it will magnify your losses. There is no free lunch here. Not recommended.

■ Covered Call Funds

They buy the stock and sell out-of-the-money call options against it for added income. The extra income this generates is not a dividend or interest—it is compensation for retaining the down-side risk of owning the stocks while giving away most of the stocks' upside. This strategy works in some historical moments and not in others. I do not recommend the funds that practice this, and I do not recommend that you try it yourself unless you are a student of options theory.

■ Master Limited Partnerships and Royalty Trusts

These structures are complicated and relatively opaque to analysis. M.L.P.s are usually involved in the delivery of natural resources (think: gas pipelines). In this respect, they are like utilities. Royalty Trusts are Canadian natural resource companies. I would not buy the individual companies here unless I were an industry analyst. Fortunately, there are now exchange-traded funds that contain a basket of these. To pick two examples, I would be comfortable holding the ALPS Alerian MLP Index ETF (ticker: AMLP) and the Guggenheim Canadian Energy and Income fund (ticker: ENY) in my income security holdings.

■ Preferred Stocks

Apart from their high yields, there is little to love about preferred stocks, either individually or wrapped in an exchange-traded fund. They are mostly from companies who have poor credit quality, and the perpetual or long-term duration of the loan makes it excessively volatile and susceptible to devastating decline in a rising interest rate environment. Look elsewhere.

■ Managed Payout Funds

I have a friend in Hollywood who made a million dollars and then one day he was broke. He had a business manager who saw to it that he received a steady income from the money while it lasted. My friend thought that he would be fine. But the manager kept paying out too much money every month until there was nothing left.

I mention this because now it has become common for funds to have a "managed distribution" policy to pay you 5 percent or 6 percent (annualized) every month, whether they have made or lost money. But why hire a fund to take your money and hand it back to you? You can do this even more economically by keeping your money in your pocket.

■ Fixed Annuities

Financial experts who are on the payrolls of insurance companies advocate fixed annuities as a cogent solution for retirees' income needs. In theory this risk pooling is a great idea, because annuities solve the problem of longevity risk by transferring money from annuitants who die early to pay for annuitants who are long-lived. In practice, though, current interest rates are so low, and the insurance companies' fees are so high, that the payout is ridiculously low.

The only kind of immediate annuity I would even consider is (a) one that is inflation-protected, (b) from a very highly rated company, (c) that I could buy directly from the insurance company without going through a commissioned insurance agent. I have heard ELM Income Group's inflation-protected annuity mentioned in this regard, but have no personal experience with them.

P.S.—Don't think that because longevity runs in your family that you are going to come out ahead. Insurance companies know that only long-lived people buy annuities and this is factored into their payout tables.

If you have no bequests, and you want to extract the highest payout from your remaining money, consider buying an immediate inflation-protected annuity directly from a highly-rated insurance company once you are in your 80s.

■ Junk Bonds

Did you ever wonder why they are called *junk* bonds? The yields are attractive, but after accounting for defaults, there is no net advantage. Graham and Dodd have the best advice here: if you are an untrained security buyer, "Do not put money in a low-grade enterprise on any terms." Their view was that an abnormally high coupon is no compensation for insufficient safety.

If you have settled on buying them anyway, at least wait until the spread between treasury bonds and junk bonds of the same maturity is wide (say, four percentage points). The fund to own is Vanguard's (ticker: VWEHX), which has a gimmick: it buys the highest rated junk bonds. Many institutional investors can only hold investment-grade bonds as a matter of policy, and they are forced to liquidate bonds that get downgraded even when it makes no sense to do so. Vanguard lies in wait to take advantage of their mistake. This is a hedge fund strategy in a bond fund wrapper. Due to the volatility of junk bonds, I would put this fund in the same category as equities. It was down over 21 percent in 2008.

■ Emerging Market Bonds

These have performed well recently, as the creditworthiness of emerging markets has surpassed that of supposedly developed countries like Italy and Spain. PowerShares Emerging Market Debt (ticker: PCY) is serviceable for one of your twenty income-oriented holdings. As with junk bonds, I would classify it with other equities. It was down 19 percent in 2008.

■ Floating Rate Income Funds

People think that floating rate income funds (Fidelity's comes to mind: ticker FFRHX) will helicopter in to save them when interest rates rise, and maybe they are right. The downside is the low credit quality of the underlying holdings. This fund was down over 16 percent in 2008—again, not exactly what one would wish for from the bond side of a portfolio. The U.S. Treasury is now considering offering floating rate bonds, which would solve the credit quality issue (we hope).

■ Business Development Companies

A grievous idea for income investors due to their super high risk. Whenever you see double-digit yields, you can dismiss the investment as too risky just on the face of it. It is like strapping a rocket pack to your back. Despite assurances from the manufacturer that it will be safe, somebody can get hurt.

■ Illiquid Investments

I do not know many individual investors who had a good experience tying up their money in illiquid investments. I know plenty of people who have had abysmal experiences. David Swensen of the Yale endowment fame has made money with private equity and venture capital funds, but Yale's experience is atypical, to say the least, and even Swensen does not recommend them for individuals without enormous sums to commit.

■ Individual Bonds

In spite of recent reforms, the bond market continues to be a fabulous way for brokers to take advantage of individual investors. With the ability to unload bonds from their own private pools at invisible bid-ask spreads, this is easy money.

The only way most people should buy individual bonds would be to buy newly minted Treasury or municipal bonds at issue. These are precisely what a broker will be least eager to sell you.

I occasionally encounter retiree income portfolios 100 percent invested in laddered municipal bonds. What's wrong with this picture? Plenty. With inflation at a "benign" annual rate of 3.5 percent, in twenty years the purchasing power of those dollars will be cut in half. Yet in twenty years, the retiree will still want to eat 3 meals a day, not 1.5 meals.

Most people are better off buying bonds using mutual funds from Vanguard. Vanguard has famously low expenses. The billions of dollars' worth of bonds they buy and sell across their bond desk means that they get razor-thin bid-ask spreads. You also get the benefit of daily liquidity. There's a lot to like about this approach.

Some people worry about the differences between owning a portfolio of individual bonds versus owning a bond fund. The net asset value of a bond mutual fund will fluctuate every day. However, so would the value of your individual bonds, if you were able to mark them to market on a daily basis. The view that individual bonds are somehow safer because you get your money back if they are held to maturity is an accounting illusion promoted by bond salesmen.

Which bond funds? A generic answer would be to divide the bond allocation between the total bond market index (ticker: BND or VBMFX) and inflation-protected bonds (ticker: VIPSX). If you want tax-free income, you could substitute intermediate-term municipal bonds (ticker: VWUIX) for the total bond index.

RISKY BUSINESS

There is a gap between what investors want and what the market delivers. Simply because retirees require a stable and high income stream does not mean that Santa Claus will supply it.

What are the risks to this portfolio? Inflation shocks are bad for almost all financial instruments, but they should be somewhat less injurious to dividend stocks than they are to growth stocks, whose prices would be discounted even more steeply. That's the theory, anyway, but that doesn't mean that is what will happen. Regulated utilities might suffer more at first, as they are squeezed between their rising borrowing costs and an inability to raise prices at will. But over time this will adjust, since by law they have to be allowed to earn a fair profit.

A steep recession would affect the value of all stocks, but these companies should be affected less. Still, if the market is down 35 percent and your stocks are down 25 percent and they have cut their dividends, you are going to feel it until the market recovers.

Two other risks could be more damaging. Rising interest rates (beyond simple inflation) would increase competition from the bond market. This hazard is imminent: many people have piled into dividend stocks in a low coupon environment as a "safe" alternative. When investors can get a 5 percent yield from supposedly safe bonds, they will dump their dividend stocks. This will likely occur during an economic expansion that raises the cost of borrowing money. Dividend stocks will immediately plunge out of favor, and the value of existing bonds will fall in the face of new bonds offering higher yields. However, nothing should threaten the existing dividends or coupons. You may not be happy, but at least you will be paid the money you were expecting. Such an event could represent a buying opportunity.

Another big danger is legislative risk. If in the future dividend tax rates are ever raised higher than capital gains tax rates at your bracket, you will have to weigh this strategy to see if it still makes sense. It might involve putting the dividend stocks in retirement accounts and capital appreciation stocks in taxable accounts. This would also have the hydraulic effect of displacing the taxable bonds presently held in retirement accounts and pushing them into municipal bonds in taxable accounts, assuming that municipal bonds retain their tax-exempt status.

I would not advise putting all your money into dividend stocks, even low-volatility ones. Once you are retired and looking to your nest egg for income, you could put most of your equity portfolio into low beta dividend stocks, and certainly you could replace all of your U.S. low beta mutual funds with these stocks. Your ability to make this shift will be constrained by your individual tax profile and the tax cost of repositioning your portfolio.

WITHDRAWAL ON THE BACK NINE

The fact that this topic continues to be debated means that there is no generally accepted solution. The method sketched here seems defensible, but clearly there are no guarantees. I vividly recall 1974, when inflation had risen 20 percent in one and a half years, the stock market had lost 40 percent of its value over the preceding two years, while bonds had fallen 35 percent. There is nothing to stop us from having 1974 again, or worse. Retirees need to put risk management ahead of fishing for yield.

For those using an income portfolio, take the coupons and dividends and spend them. Following the process outlined in this chapter, the yield should be over 4 percent. If it is closer to 5 percent, pocket some of the cash in a reserve fund for a rainy day.

The old school teaching is that we ought to live off the interest and dividends from our investments and never dig into principal. Eating into principal is immoral, in this view. Unfortunately, not many baby boomers—even affluent ones—can afford to follow this creed. There won't be enough money in the kitty for the dividends and coupons alone to sustain them through their prolonged and expensive retirements. If the demographic trend of an aging population proves to be bad for the stock market (as the former Mouseketeers all seek to cash in their holdings at the same time), a dividend-based approach to retirement income should work better than one relying on capital appreciation.

For those investing for total returns, overweight your equity portfolio toward U.S. low beta stocks during your late working/early retirement years. Both the income and the capital appreciation strategies emphasize low beta investing during these years. Your portfolio has to carry you for 30 or 40 years. This argues for a conservative allocation (and a low payout) precisely when you are most active and could use the extra money. All the schemes to raise your payout here involve higher risks or conjecture that you will spend less money in late retirement. While you may not be kiteboarding in Waikiki during your 90s, your recreation budget could easily be surpassed by cascading out-of-pocket health care costs during your final years. Obamacare health review (AKA "death") panels will not want to pay for expensive treatments for old people who will soon be going to Elvisville, when prescribing medical marijuana is so much more cost-effective. My impression is that having ready money comes in handy at any age.

In a study I did of retirement withdrawal rates, I noticed that the portfolios where people got into trouble were those where they suffered crucial setbacks in early retirement. This forces people to either sell equities at distressed levels to cover their living expenses, or double down on equities in a perilous environment by selling from the fixed income side of the portfolio. Neither option is particularly enticing, but the bigger mistake—at least, so far—has been to sell stocks when they are down. It has worked better to sell the bonds in order to give the stocks time to recover.

In Ben's and my book on retirement, we recommended that retirees recalculate their withdrawal rate every five years, since at that point, presumably, we have five years fewer to live. This lets us withdraw more over the shorter period that remains with the same degree of safety. Prof. John Spitzer researched our proposal in the *Financial Services Review*, and concluded that periodically adjusting the withdrawal rate both increased the amount withdrawn and decreased the likelihood of running out of money. Assume that you will live to 100 and plug your specifics into a website like www.firecalc.com. If you do this every five years, you will see how you can raise your allowance, gradually at first, then a lot more later. Alternatively, you can keep your withdrawals constant and increase your equity allocation at the same expected degree of safety.

OTHER RETIREMENT CONSIDERATIONS

Once you retire, you will want to move to Vancouver, Washington. This way you can live in a state with no income tax, and drive across the bridge to shop in Portland, Oregon—a state with no sales tax. Or, move to Puerto Rico, where you will have an all-in tax bill of 7 percent.

However, you won't. You'll keep living right where you are now, close to family and friends. At most you will downsize to a deluxe condominium that will end up costing exactly what your current house does. Your kids will be mad at you for selling "their" house.

After you retire, you will have better and cheaper investment options if you roll over your 401k to an IRA. If you have a pension plan and they are offering a lump sum payout, you will have to make a calculated decision. To find out if it is a good deal, compare what you could get by reinvesting the lump sum in a highly-rated annuity (http://www.brkdirect.com/spia/EZquote.asp) versus accepting what the pension's annuity will pay you. You will discover that the highly rated annuity pays you significantly less. This is a reflection of the credit risk you assume by staying within your pension plan. Up to $4,125/month will be guaranteed by the Pension Benefit Guaranty Association; after that, you're on your own. The dilemma is worse for high-earning women, who can take advantage of mandated unisex annuity pricing within their plan, but must face actuarial pricing (= a lower payment) if they annuitize their lump sum payout elsewhere. Fortunately, there is always the option of investing the payout and not going the annuity route at all. You will have to weigh the particulars of your situation.

A simple rule of thumb can extend the value of your nest egg during withdrawal. Don't rebalance your portfolio first and then draw it down from each side; instead, draw down each side to rebalance your portfolio. Example: you started the year at 40 percent stocks and 60 percent bonds. Stocks had a bad year, and by December your portfolio is pitched at 35 percent stocks and 65 percent bonds. Sell down the bonds to take your annual withdrawal that year, and then rebalance the remainder back to the 40/60 allocation. If you harvest your portfolio two years in advance of your need to spend the money, you should have a meaningful cash cushion and will have more flexibility on the timing of your portfolio withdrawals so you won't need to liquidate assets when the stock market lies in wreckage.

Apply for Social Security in whatever way optimizes your

family's projected lifetime payout. Because of the tremendous value of the inflation-indexed annuity and the high rate (7–8 percent annually) at which it grows from ages 66 to 70, you will be better insured if you wait until age 70 to begin receiving benefits. However, there are a number of permutations. Given the dollars at stake, navigate to one of the online calculators that—for a small fee—provide a robust analysis of your best tactic (http://socialsecuritysolutions.com or http://www.maximizemysocialsecurity. com).

Finally, if you want to maximize your standard of living in retirement, be aware that your domicile is a valuable asset. If you sell your pyramid and rent, you will have far more liquidity than if you hang on and it goes into your estate. Against this, you may leave a smaller estate for your heirs, and you will have the psychic costs that go with being a renter rather than being an owner.

Chapter Eight: A Hitchhiker's Guide to Asset Protection

The thoughts of others
Were light and fleeting,
Of lovers' meeting
Or luck or fame.
Mine were of trouble,
And mine were steady,
So I was ready
When trouble came

—A.E. Housman

Here is how to protect yourself:

Buy a farm. One near a small town filled with friendly neighbors. Not close to any large, rioting city or downwind from nuclear fallout from the (former) city. Your farm has its own source of water. You have stored lots of tinned food, seed, ammunition, gold coins, gasoline, and medical supplies there.

One of your sons, who lives there, is a farmer. Another son, an Army Ranger, lives in the nearby town, as does his wife, an emergency physician.

In the barn, you keep your Cessna Citation and drums of aviation fuel. You are a pilot, and this will take your family to the other farm you maintain in another country, should the worst happen here.

Since you will decamp to your farm at the first alarm, you should be reasonably safe. Congratulations!

While this kind of end-of-civilization scenario vividly commands our attention, the more probable risks to your security and peace-of-mind are much closer to home. In fact, the main danger to your assets is…you.

We have already seen how a couple of ill-considered mouse clicks have the power to erase decades of returns from your investment portfolio. However, you are also a danger to the human capital that underlies your financial capital. You are in danger from high-risk health behavior like smoking and lack of exercise and obesity and failing to get proper medical care when indicated. Steve Jobs might have lived longer if he hadn't chosen to dabble in "new age" approaches to liver cancer. Then there are all the reckless behaviors that human beings are prey to: gambling, drinking, drugs, speeding, bad companions, and so forth. There are periods of inordinate stress in everyone's lives when they act in ways that are functionally crazy, even if they do not normally belong in the one quarter of the population that psychiatrists say carry a diagnosable mental illness. Let's take all these issues off the table. Let's assume that you are A-OK along all of these dimensions.

Are you high net worth? Then by definition you are at high risk. You are not getting paid six or seven figures to work as a street mime. Your actions have important consequences, and given the law of large numbers, not everyone is going to be happy with everything you do.

We have already mentioned how financial predators target people with assets. The best frauds do not seem fraudulent at all. They are investment schemes that you want to get in, just like Mercedes knows what you want in a car and the Four Seasons knows what you like in a hotel room. Bernie Madoff is an obvious example. (By the way, he now advises his fellow prison inmates to invest in index funds. Perhaps I should have called this book, *The Bernie*

Madoff Investment Method....?). We have advised you to custody your assets somewhere big and safe and suggested that you follow a well-trod investment strategy. Finally, we have advised you to steer clear of even honest and well-meaning brokers and investment advisors who are friendly and confident but are nonetheless tools in a grand design by the financial services industry to take your dreams and make them their own.

As I review my list of clients, I can recall examples where they were made victims of extortion, even though in every case they did nothing wrong. The bitter truth is, once you are high net worth, you wear a bull's-eye on your back. Greedy, envious people want what you have, because it is a straighter crooked path to wealth than having to earn the money themselves.

Imagine that you come to the office one morning and find a registered letter from a well-known attorney waiting for you. In it, the attorney relates that she represents a young woman who works for the same company you do. Several weeks ago, the narrative continues, you were working late and molested her. Before she sues you and your firm, though, she is giving you an opportunity to make a financial settlement that will allow her to put the whole incident behind her and get on with her life. She is asking for $1,000,000.

What do you do? Now that you think about it, you realize that the bedrock on which your entire life rests is your reputation. Once word gets out, most people simply will project their own guilty consciences on to you and assume you are guilty. They will never look at you in the same way again. Your professional life will be severely compromised, and it won't be very pleasant for your family, either.

Do you fight it, or go to arbitration and perhaps get off the hook for a quiet hundred thousand dollar settlement? It is a tough call. This kind of shakedown is not an aberration; it is a business model. You might think that this only happens in a made-for-TV movie, but it can happen to nice people like you.

Here is more bad news. The next greatest danger to you comes from those nearest to you. The Trojan Horse is already inside your compound. By this, I mean your family and the people who work for them.

Your spouse: nothing erases a fortune faster than divorce. Start by dividing your money in three: one for you, one for her, and one for the attorneys. A pre- or post-nuptial agreement will make this dreadful process less unpleasant if the worst happens. At the very least, a properly-worded document can help shield you if you live in a community property state and one of you is sued.

Your kids: Imagine that your 16-year-old son gets drunk at a party and gets in a serious traffic accident causing multiple severe, lifelong injuries. (Thank heavens you never did anything irresponsible when you were his age....) Remember the first axiom of the personal injury lawyer: if something bad happens, it's somebody's fault. And the second is like unto it: the more money, the more guilty.

There's more. Did I mention that your daughter's Facebook page is studded with personal information about your family that would be unduly interesting to criminals? They can find out everything they want to know about your family from websites like Spokeo and SafetyWeb for a few dollars. Then there's your oldest son. His greedy wife wants to divorce him and she feels entitled to a big slice of the pie. Not to mention, there's an excellent chance that your too-clever children will eventually run your family business into the ground, destroying your life's work and legacy.

Your parents: thirty states have filial dependency laws. If your parents are in a nursing home racking up some big unpaid bills, those institutions can come after you for the money. You have the right to pay.

Your help: because you trust them, they have enormous capacity to harm you. This could be accidental, like the contractor who falls off the roof. Or it could be malicious, like the handyman who clones the contents of your hard drive. It could also be your business partner, attorney, accountant, financial advisor, or doctor, any of whom might harm you even while acting with the best of intentions.

GENERAL PRINCIPLES OF ASSET PROTECTION

Naturally, you'd like to do something about these kinds of scenarios. Yet a lot of asset protection is itself a scam. Attorney Jay Adkisson, who wrote the book on the subject, spends many of his hours trying to undo the damage done by other attorneys who foist asset protection schemes on the public. The last thing you ever want to do is go to a "seminar" advertising asset protection techniques, even if lunch is included. People looking for asset protection are frequent targets for getting ripped off. It's far more expensive to retain an attorney to fix a problem than it is to hire one to set it up correctly in the first place.

I am going to mention some fundamental safeguards for you to consider. I am not an attorney and I don't play one on TV (although I was a judge once on the reality TV show *America's Most Smartest Model*), so this is not legal advice. If you want to set up a custom asset protection plan, there is no harm in getting two opinions from reputable attorneys in the field. I can't tell you whether you need a Family Limited Partnership on the Isle of Man or a Nevis LLC. Often what passes for asset protection is an excuse to promote expensive special-purpose insurance policies. These may have a place in someone's universe, but I wonder if that person is really you.

Carefully weigh the trade-offs between asset protection, estate planning, taxes, and the overall expense of setting up and maintaining whatever apparatus you put in place versus the actuarial probability of the risks you face. These stars do not always, or even often, align.

The first principle of asset protection is that it should be done in advance of a "claim," which is something that gives rise to a liability—such as taking a loan or getting into a car accident. Once you've got the letter from the attorney suing you for a million dollars, it's too late to be thinking about that bank account in the Cayman Islands or selling all your worldly goods to your brother for $1. The killer issue is "fraud in the conveyance." That is, if a judge feels that you are moving assets around to avoid paying what you owe, he will order you to undo the transactions. Then your assets will be available for carving up like a Christmas goose. You will comply, because you won't like the alternative, which is you sitting in jail.

The second idea is that asset protection should be done in the course of doing things that you ordinarily would do anyway as part of your prudent, long-term financial planning. You want to have these structures in place years before trouble arrives, so it doesn't look like you are doing some suspicious tap dancing to avoid taking responsibility for your actions. Everything should be transparent, because you have nothing to hide. You never do anything purely for "asset protection," because that would imply that you wanted to avoid paying creditors what they are owed. Instead you want to do financial planning, estate planning, tax planning, fiduciary planning, etc. You want to have a clear paper trail displaying what you did, when you did it, and a story to tell the judge explaining your actions.

The third idea is that asset protection is not so much about putting all your assets into a Kryptonite box as it is about creating an atmosphere where attacking them will take a lot of time and trouble, and so will motivate your creditors to seek a prompt resolution of their claims on reasonable terms.

Here are some structures that anyone can use for basic asset protection. These simple measures are inexpensive and offer a high order of utility and cost-efficiency. Even so, they were good enough to protect O.J.

Note: under a number of the headings below you will find a list of states, because asset protections vary widely from state to state. These recitations of state names may fracture the mellifluous flow of the prose, but this information is not always easy to track down, so I wanted to memorialize it here. Laws can change, though, so double-check it before taking action.

INSURANCE

Insurance is your first line of defense. The beauty of insurance is that it creates a juicy target for a plaintiff's attorney that allows both of you to quickly settle the case and move on with your lives. Of course you will buy a high-coverage auto insurance policy and have a homeowner's or renter's policy to shield you from liability. Five million dollars in umbrella coverage should carry you through one horrifying auto accident. I would consider that amount the minimum coverage for most high-net-worth individuals. Ten million dollars would be better. When I look at how much money I spend on different types of insurance every year—homeowner's, umbrella, professional liability, health, auto, disability, life, long-term care, etc., I nearly faint. Nevertheless, I take off the rubber band and consider it money well spent. Of all of these, the one you are most likely to skimp on is disability insurance, which is inherently expensive due to the high potential for fraud, but you should consider it anyway because disability is one of the higher actuarial risks that you face. Financial planning software can calculate the exact amount of term life insurance you should buy, but the rough rule is four to seven times your annual salary. When you can afford to self-insure, self-insurance is always the cheapest.

If you are called upon to serve on a board of directors of some little agency or non-profit, make sure they have directors' and officers' liability insurance with appropriate limits. When the president's secretary sues him, s/he will name you personally in the lawsuit as well, because you have money and because the board failed to exercise proper supervision and thereby implicitly condoned the hostile and sexist work environment. When people tell me that their rector or pastor was fired for sleeping with a member of the congregation, not only am I no longer shocked, I now assume it was in the job description.

Another point: don't keep a million dollars parked in your bank checking account. Federal Deposit Insurance Corporation (FDIC) insurance will only shelter $250,000. You either need to have several carefully titled accounts to game the system, or you should pack the money off to Treasurydirect.gov, where it will be safely kept in T-bills, or you should send it to the CDARS program at BNY Mellon, where they can farm out virtually any amount to a number of CD accounts across the country, each under the limit. You may not know anyone who kept a million dollars in the bank and then got a check from the FDIC for only $100,000 when the bank failed, but it has happened.

LIMITED LIABILITY COMPANIES

Holding your assets in the correct type of structure is another basic form of asset protection. When you buy a vacation home that you also intend to rent, don't buy it in your own name. Put it inside a limited liability company (LLC), a business entity that protects owners to some degree from the acts and debts of the business. If your spouse wants to sell cupcakes, make sure the company has a corporate structure so your spouse is not opening a side-door that puts all your assets at risk.

Not all states are equal in the creditor protections they provide. You ideally want to form your LLC in a state that only allows what are called "charging orders" as remedies for creditors: Alabama, Alaska, Arizona, Delaware, Florida, Hawaii, Idaho, Illinois, Kansas, Maine, Michigan, Minnesota, Mississippi, Nevada, New Jersey, North Dakota, Ohio, Oklahoma, Pennsylvania, South Dakota, Tennessee, Texas, Virginia, and Wyoming. "Charging orders" mean that creditors have a right to economic distributions from the company, but are not given voting rights or ownership in the company itself. Thus, they may receive a tax obligation for their claim, yet not receive any money to actually pay the tax bill. That prospect can discourage them from attacking you.

The laws that will govern are those of the state that you are in, so there is no point in establishing an out-of-state LLC since you will be unable to avail yourself of its protections when you need them. Give your LLC a pleasant name from a map of the English countryside, like Windermere Park LLC. Then, when your tenant slips in the shower and decides it was your fault, his lawyer will look at the agreement and tell him that it's not going to be worth his while to sue.

An LLC will not protect you from your own negligence. It will not do you much good to have your car in an LLC. There, your first line of defense is insurance.

Delaware, Nevada, and Wyoming all explicitly protect single-member LLCs the same way they protect multi-member LLCs. If you open an LLC in other states, it should not have just a single member if you want to maintain the optimum level of protection. Sell a five or ten percent stake to your spouse or child for fair market value and see that they receive all the ongoing benefits owed them as a result (such as any distributions you make to shareholders). Even the most obtuse judge will grasp the concept of fiduciary responsibility.

Whatever the corporate structure, it is important that you take a regular salary out of your company, rather than pulling out cash on an ad hoc basis. Garnishments only will take 25 percent of your salary, after withholding. Your salary can't be protected if there is no regular salary to begin with, though.

RETIREMENT ACCOUNTS

Why was O.J. able to retire to a comfortable life in Florida (at least initially) despite having a $33.5 million civil judgment against him for the wrongful death of Nicole Simpson? In part, it was because his NFL pension was immune from attack by creditors.

So is yours. About the only good thing that can be said about 401k plans is that they have wonderful asset protection stipulations, and IRAs are often nearly as good. The law doesn't care if you are young and destitute; it just doesn't want you to be old and destitute. While 401ks and IRAs are protected in bankruptcy up to $1 million and sometimes more in the case of rollovers, the level of protection from other creditors varies widely from state to state. In my tour of the country, I was saddened to learn that Alabama, Arkansas, California, Idaho, Maine, Massachusetts, Minnesota, Nebraska, Nevada, New Jersey, North Dakota, Oregon, Pennsylvania, South Dakota, and Virginia did not have explicit substantial protections for IRAs. This leads to a dilemma between the asset protection vs. investment perspectives. If you hold a 401k plan, a defined benefit plan, or some other ERISA plan and you reside in one of these states, you could be better off keeping your money in that plan for asset protection. From an investment position, you would be better off rolling the plan over to an IRA, where your investment options would be cheaper and more plentiful. It will all come down to particular cases: your desire for this level of protection, your state's provisions, and the expenses and investment choices within your 401k plan.

HOMESTEAD

Homestead laws were originally designed to prevent people from losing their homes to creditors. It looked bad when widows were thrown out on the street after their husbands died. Sadly, the amounts protected have not been indexed for inflation over the years, so the protections in most states have become trivial. No homestead exemption will defend you from the claims of your mortgage lender, the IRS, or an ex-spouse. Arkansas, Kansas, Florida, Texas, Iowa, Oklahoma, South Dakota, and the District of Columbia have the best protections, with Nevada close behind. O.J. was able to buy a house in Florida and shelter the entire value from attachment. You have to meet residency requirements in order to take advantage of these protections, and you need to establish your homestead 40 months before filing for bankruptcy.

If you live in a state that offers substantial homestead protection, you are better off owning your house outright. If you live in a state without much in the way of homestead protections, you are better off carrying a large mortgage, and buying an annuity to cover the mortgage payment—at least for asset protection purposes (but note that there would be frictional costs in doing this). A Home Equity Line of Credit (HELOC) could be another means of quickly extracting equity from your house. This technique—called *equity stripping*—has many uses for asset protection in business, but will require consultation with an attorney who is expert in this area.

529 PLANS

As with retirement accounts, education savings 529 plans set up for your children or grandchildren are also protected species. Contributions that have been resting in these accounts for three years will be beyond the reach of bankruptcy courts. Protection from creditors outside of bankruptcy varies with state law. You can make a prorated one-time, 5-year gift of $65,000 per person to these plans ($130,000 for a married couple) without triggering federal gift tax.

Investment-wise, most of these plans aren't very good. Among the few plans worth considering, Ohio's CollegeAdvantage 529 Savings Plan has the best combination of protection from creditors ("variable college savings program account(s) shall not be subject to execution, garnishment, attachment, the operation of bankruptcy or the insolvency laws, or other process of law") and low fees (about 0.25 percent annually for Vanguard's Moderate Age-Based Option). Residents of any state can participate in Ohio's plan, which offers a cheap, set-it-and-forget-it solution. While 529 plans are nominally for the purpose of paying for college expenses, the owner (you are the owner; the kid is the beneficiary) can always pull money out for any non-educational endeavor, provided you are willing to pay taxes plus a 10 percent penalty on earnings.

Pennsylvania, Arizona, Maine, Missouri, and Kansas let you deduct contributions to any state's 529 plan on your state's income tax. Many other states offer tax deductions for residents, provided residents use their state's own (dismal, often) plans: Alabama, Arizona, Connecticut, Idaho, Illinois, Indiana, Iowa, Louisiana, Maine,

Maryland, Michigan, Mississippi, Nebraska, New York, North Carolina, North Dakota, Ohio, Oklahoma, Utah, Vermont, Virginia, D.C., West Virginia, and Wisconsin. In these cases, I would be tempted to donate to my own state's plan, take the tax deduction, then wait a year and transfer the account to the Ohio plan mentioned above, unless there is some reason why my state would disallow this.

Tenants in Entirety

Some states (Delaware, D.C., Florida, Hawaii, Indiana, Maryland, Massachusetts, Michigan, North Carolina, Ohio, Pennsylvania, Tennessee, Vermont, Virginia, and Wyoming) allow for a form of joint ownership called *tenancy by the entirety*. This means that a husband and wife can own the property as a marital asset. If either the husband or the wife is sued separately, his or her individual interest cannot be withdrawn from it, since it belongs to the marriage. Of course, if both parties are sued, then the property does come into play, as it could in the event of death or divorce. The IRS also will be happy to crack it open to get at back taxes owed by either party. A trade-off is that this form of ownership traps the asset inside your estate for tax purposes. For your home, an alternative method could be to use a Qualified Personal Residence Trust, which could shield the asset while removing it from your estate entirely.

If you live in a community property state, the first step toward protecting half your assets is a post-nuptial agreement commuting community property to separate property, preferably with the more liquid half going to the spouse who is less likely to be sued. Prenuptial agreements are even immune from the "fraud in the conveyance" statutes, although you may be jumping from the frying pan into the fire if divorce ensues.

LIFE INSURANCE & ANNUITIES

While I am not in love with whole life insurance policies or most annuities, they do have a role in asset protection. The exemptions for life insurance and annuities vary tremendously from state-to-state, both in what is protected and the amount. Some states protect the cash value from the creditors of the owners, while other states only protect the death benefit from the creditors of the beneficiary, and the remaining states fall somewhere in between. There are also complications if one buys a policy in one state and then moves to another state, or if the death benefit goes to a child in still another state. In many cases, payments to the beneficiary of a policy (spouse or child, for example) are protected, but not payments to the owner of the policy. In others, there is weasel language allowing "payment necessary for the support of debtor," but you and the person suing you will have different ideas of what dollar amount corresponds to that language. One upside to all this confusion is that even if you buy a policy in a state where it is not protected, you could move to a state where it is protected if you are sued.

Many states put low limits on the amount backstopped. My survey of the field suggests that Arizona, Florida, Kentucky, Michigan, New Mexico, Oklahoma, and Texas have the broadest protections for life insurance, while Florida, Maryland, Michigan, New Mexico, Oklahoma, and Texas have the strongest protections for annuities. Because fees and commissions for these products are often extremely high, I would not buy them unless I had a major concern for asset protection, I lived in a state where those protections were respected, and I could purchase the policy directly from a low-fee insurer rather than going through a commissioned agent. Vanguard, Fidelity, and TIAA-CREF would be on my short list for annuities, as would USAA if I had military service on my resume, adding ELM Income to the list if I were looking for an inflation-indexed immediate annuity, which is the only kind of fixed annuity I ordinarily would buy.

Then there is the question of who guarantees the guarantee. I know what a guarantee means when I buy a toaster. I'm a little hazier on what it means when I hand an insurance company a check for a million dollars. What if the company paying your immediate annuity goes out of business? Insurance companies invest in the same waters that everyone else does; they have no magic access to an alternative universe of positive investment returns. Historically they have been unlikely to fail, but asset protection is precisely about making provisions for worst-case scenarios. Insurance companies are regulated at the state level. Your state promises to guarantee them, but only to a certain limit, which is almost invariably $300,000 for all lines of insurance, and as low as $100,000 for a single policy. You will have to verify these limits with your state guaranty association. It might be smarter to buy three $100,000 annuities than one $300,000 annuity, for example. Your state's finances are probably overseen by chuckleheads, while your insurance company's finances are run by Harvard MBAs, making it an intriguing question which will go bankrupt first.

PERSONAL SECURITY

While we're on the subject of asset protection, may I inject a note on the subject of personal security? I have several clients who have been held up in their homes by men with guns. It doesn't matter how nice a person you are; if you have money, you are a potential target. That big picture window in your living room is like a Neiman Marcus catalog to a thief. Whether or not you own and know how to use firearms, at a minimum you owe it to yourself to download one of the home security checklists available on the Internet and inspect your property from a burglar's lynx-eyed view.

Video cameras do more good than the occasional drive-by from a rent-a-cop armed with a cheeseburger. Here's another tip from Dick Tracy's crimestopper's textbook: don't keep your automobile registration in the glove compartment or have your home address programmed into your GPS, because if someone steals your car, they'll know where you live and have your garage door opener, too.

Every region of the country is prone to some kind of major calamity, and if one hits near you, you will be glad to have taken precautions. Maintain sufficient supplies on the premises to get you through three to seven days without public services. You also want to have a digital video record of your possessions and all of your important papers and photos securely backed up online. If ATM machines aren't working, you will be glad to have a stash of cash hidden somewhere. Finally, keep a "grab & go" bag in reach in case you need to clear out fast.

Create a family plan to deal with the most probable emergencies that might arise. There is material on these topics on the World Wide Web, so I won't rehash it. If you have not made adequate provision for these circumstances, there is scarcely a better use of your next weekend. You will sleep better even if misfortune never comes.

When you bring someone in to your family's circle of trust—maid, driver, dog walker, pretty much anyone—do a background check and ring up their references. Don't lend out house keys unless they can't be copied (Medeco). Your nanny might seem nice, but what about her doper boyfriend whom you've never met? It is difficult to know whom to trust when you are high-net-worth, because immoral people can deliberately insinuate themselves into your orbit for the purpose of taking advantage of you, and even good people can turn to the dark side if a sufficient temptation presents itself. The threshold that can lure people into criminal behavior is undoubtedly lower than you think. Lexis-Nexis will give you their legal histories (driving and criminal records, for example) for a nominal fee. People become militant about taking precautions after they have a problem; the secret is to take precautions before then.

Keep a low profile and do not showcase your wealth. There are enormous intractable structural problems in the U.S. economy, including an $86 trillion dollar off-the-books shortfall in dedicated Social Security and Medicare spending. While we all hope to muddle through, there is no assurance that everything will end happily. Rich people are a perennial target and convenient scapegoat. If we have major civil unrest, it will be great to have a bolt-hole to lie low for a while. That farm with a water supply far away from the big city might not be such a bad idea after all, if you can afford it. What are the odds? Who knows? Let's say there is a five percent chance of social upheaval in the U.S. during your lifetime. If five percent of your assets could buy you some critical protection in the worst case, it might be worth considering. However, human beings are generally inept at both estimating and preparing for historical low-probability events. Just when you think you are safe in the bombshelter, an asteroid arrives from outer space.

Chapter Nine: Minimizing Taxes

*"Any one may so arrange his affairs that his taxes shall
be as low as possible; he is not bound to choose that
pattern which will best pay the Treasury; there is not
even a patriotic duty to increase one's taxes."*

—Learned Hand

While we might hope that there are tax tricks of the millionaires that can make a monkey out of the Internal Revenue Service, this is generally not true (unless you run a hedge fund or a private equity fund). Getting a letter from the IRS is not like getting a stern letter from the club secretary. They mean business. If you are only high-net-worth (as opposed to ultra-high-net-worth), you don't have enough money to fight them.

This subject is as big as the tax code itself. I'm not a CPA, so I will just highlight a few stray notions that strike my fancy, with the idea that you will take these up with your own tax professional. I am an investment guy, so my emphasis will be on the investing angles. If the 2013 changes in the tax law prescribe a different course of action from that presented here, I will update my views under the link to this book on my website, www.phildemuth.com.

INVESTMENT ACCOUNTS

One thing that would be really useful is a stable tax code. However unfair a tax code might be—and any tax code will seem unfair to someone—at least it would allow for long-term planning. We would all complain about the parts we didn't like and then try to work around them as best we could. However, that is not what we have. The tax code exists in a world of Heraclitan flux, such that you cannot dip your toe into the same provision twice. The basic idea is for it to be as complicated as possible so that politicians can sell exemptions in exchange for campaign contributions.

Given a future fraught with legislative uncertainty, there is an argument for presenting a diversified tax picture to the taxing authorities. If all your money is tied up in one type of investment account, that type of account might be taxed hardest of all. Diversification means keeping money in taxable, tax-deferred, and tax-exempt accounts.

Your assets normally have two owners: you, and your Uncle Sam. You and he share the wealth. For taxable accounts, your portion is the balance less the short- and long-term capital gains taxes you will pay when you sell them. If you can postpone withdrawing appreciated assets until departure time, your heirs get a stepped-up cost basis (after paying any estate taxes). With your tax-deferred accounts like IRAs and 401ks, Uncle Sam's share is your marginal tax rate when you pull the money out. Only your tax-exempt Roth accounts are truly yours (unless Congress changes the law).

ASSET LOCATION

There is general agreement that tax-efficient assets belong in taxable accounts and tax-inefficient assets belong in tax-sheltered accounts. The guidance is that stocks go in your taxable accounts and bonds go in your IRA/401k. Let's fine-tune this.

Roth accounts usually have the least headroom and are the most valuable. Because of their potential for long-term tax-exempt growth, the ideal Roth asset has high growth prospects. To me, that spells Emerging Market equities and small/value or momentum stocks, and Real Estate Investment Trusts.

Tax-deferred accounts are great for any asset classes that threaten to issue a K-1 partnership income schedule form at tax time. Commodity funds like GLD (gold) or DBC (Deutsche Bank Commodity Index Fund) are examples, as are any master limited partnerships. You rarely would have to worry about getting a K-1 if the fund is held in a tax-deferred account. Next, consider Treasury Inflation-Protected Securities (TIPS), because these can potentially generate phantom income (income on which you will be taxed this year but not actually receive until some future date). High yield bonds and emerging market bonds (if any) also belong in tax-deferred accounts. Finally, put the rest of your taxable bonds here, to the extent that you have room. You always have the option of buying municipal bonds if part of your bond allocation spills out into your taxable account. Equities kept in tax-deferred accounts convert long-term capital gains into ordinary income upon withdrawal. Depending on your tax bracket in retirement, that may not be a good idea.

Index funds have the lowest expenses and are the most tax-efficient, since they have the lowest turnover. Want to find out how tax efficient/inefficient your funds are? Cruise over to Morningstar.com, punch in your fund's ticker, and then go to the little tab labeled "Tax." There you will see two statistics of special interest: its "Tax Cost Ratio" and its "Potential Cap Gains Exposure." The Tax Cost Ratio is how much of the total return is lost to taxes on an annualized basis. Lower is better. If the number is high, consider putting the fund in a tax-deferred account. You also might prefer a fund with lower embedded Capital Gains to one that has more, other things equal, which they never are.

If international stock funds are put into a taxable account, you have the hope of reclaiming the foreign tax credit (for taxes paid abroad). This tax credit would be foregone were the funds held tax-qualified accounts. Of course, you will have to pay your accountant to file a special form to claim it. There may be a tiny marginal benefit to doing this if you claim the tax credit. If you aren't going to bother, it will be less expensive to house the foreign stocks in a tax-deferred account in the first place.

RETIREMENT ACCOUNTS

According to the study by Kotlikoff and Rapson (2005), there is a tremendous lifetime benefit to contributing to 401k and IRA accounts for high-income families. Table 9.1 summarizes their findings for various families (at the then-prevailing tax rates).

Table 9.1: Additional Payback per $1 Invested			
Traditional IRA/401k			
	Household Income		
Age	**100K**	**200K**	**500K**
30	$0.20	$0.54	$1.55
45	$0.21	$0.44	$0.80
60	$0.36	$0.48	$0.49
Roth IRA/401k			
	Household Income		
Age	**100K**	**200K**	**500K**
30	$0.19	$0.33	$1.22
45	$0.18	$0.31	$0.57
60	$0.25	$0.24	$0.28

Especially for young high-earners, these accounts are a money machine. This is one of the few hiccups in the tax code that favors the high-net-worth, so take advantage of the opportunity.

When you roll your 401k into an IRA, and you hold employee stock purchased with pretax contributions and employee matches, you have a calculation to make. The tax code allows you to break out your employee stock separately, pay income tax on its cost basis at your marginal rate, and then pay capital gains taxes on any amount over that when the stock is finally sold. If you roll the stock into an IRA, all of the proceeds will be taxed at marginal rates when they are pulled out. If capital gains rates are lower than your marginal rates at the time the stock is sold, breaking out the employee stock separately will prove to be a better deal.

ROTH CONVERSIONS

When the government, strapped for cash, finally let people earning $100,000+ convert their Traditional IRAs to Roths and pay taxes on the conversion amount, a Who concert-like stampede into Roth IRAs was expected. This didn't happen. The questions surrounding the value of making a conversion were tricky enough to give investors pause, especially with the certainty of a large tax bill up front. What confounds the analysis is the unknown variable of future tax rates. In theory, if you think that your tax rates today are lower than they will be when you eventually pull the money out of your Traditional IRA, and you can afford to pay the taxes out of other funds so you don't have to deplete your overall tax-deferred savings in the process, the conversion can be a good idea. But are you willing to convert a million dollar IRA to a Roth if it means writing a check to the U.S. Treasury for $400,000 today? I thought not.

Roth conversions make sense for people who don't need the money. If you are unlikely to ever touch the Roth money in retirement and you have bequest motives, the conversion becomes attractive, since there are no mandatory distributions during your lifetime. Your children can inherit your Roth and (after paying estate taxes) withdraw the money tax-free amortized over their expected life spans, while it compounds tax-free decade after decade. Against this, some people fear that our future revenue-starved government will look to rich people to pay their "fair share" of taxes and tax their Roth income anyway.

Another case worth considering: a Roth conversion is a good idea if it can be done on the cheap. If you have any year where you are not paying taxes, jam up and jelly tight and convert your IRA to a Roth up to one of the lower tax bracket limits. You can do Roth conversions at any age, which means that you can build your Roth balance by making small conversions over time (say, after you retire and your income has fallen).

A daring idea for a backdoor Roth was popularized by Ashlea Eberling in *Forbes* Magazine. She proposes funding a non-deductible Traditional IRA with post-tax dollars ($5,000 annually, or $6,000 if you are over 50). Wait until you have a brokerage statement for your files with the new Traditional IRA, and then convert it to a Roth, tax-free. This may not sound like much money to the affluent, but if you do this year after year and let the money compound it can grow to a tidy sum over time.

(One wrinkle: the *pro rata rule*, which says that you must consider the value of all your IRAs when paying tax on the conversion. If you have $95,000 in a Traditional IRA, and you convert your new $5,000 nondeductible IRA to a Roth, you will be taxed as if the conversion were 95 percent taxable. Even here, however, there is a workaround. Fold your pretax IRA back into your 401k (called a "roll-in"—research whether your plan will accept this). That way, your post tax IRA becomes your only IRA, and you can proceed with the conversion unhindered.)

Having different types of accounts gives you the ability to fine-tune your taxable income during retirement. For example, you can pull out enough from your Traditional IRA to take you to the top of your current tax bracket, take money from your taxable accounts as needed thereafter, and keep withdrawals from your Roth IRAs to a minimum.

DEFINED BENEFIT PLANS

The defined benefit plan lives! It's not for everybody, and you have to create it yourself. They are for high-earning, older professionals or small business owners who are either sole proprietors or who have a few young, much less well-compensated employees. Typically, these are physicians, dentists, CPAs, or realtors with stable income streams. They also might be appropriate for someone who gets a W-2 but who regularly does consulting, speaking, or writing on the side, and would like to shelter that income. You need to have enough disposable business income to fund the plan every year, and this is additional money you want to set aside after funding your other retirement accounts. The money doesn't even have to come from your business; you can redeploy other assets that you want to move to tax-deferred status. The older you are, the more you can contribute.

When I heard of these plans, I was scared of being shackled to making large, fixed annual contributions and then having to buy an annuity at the end. The requirements turn out to be far less onerous than I thought.

First, you hire a (low fee) actuary to set up and administer the plan. The plan is tailored to you and your business. It will require you to make a fixed annual contribution every year. The key is that this contribution is fully tax-deductible. If you put in $100,000, then your business earns $100,000 less that year. This amounts to a ~$40,000 valentine to you from the IRS. Your contribution goes into an account at a custodian of your choice, like Vanguard, Fidelity, TD Ameritrade, or Schwab, with full access to the range of funds they provide (or that your advisor can provide if he is on the account). You control the investments. There's no annuity. Ideally, the account is invested in something that does not provide wild swings in asset value (bonds?) and so does not encounter unexpected issues with under- or over-funding. You have the option of setting a low mandatory contribution and then making bonus contributions during good years. You are not locked into any rigid payment schedule.

You have to pay a (tax-deductible) fee every year to the administrator for the ongoing actuarial calculation to ensure the account is appropriately funded. The plan has to include all employees who meet the criteria for inclusion, but ideally will be designed so that the lion's share goes to you. The plan has a ticking clock attached—it closes in five, seven, or ten years, or whenever you set it.

At that point, you roll the plan over into an IRA. In effect, your personal defined benefit plan is like a super IRA. Instead of saving $5,000 annually, though, as with a traditional IRA, you can put in six-figure sums. By the way, there's no law that says you can't fund an IRA, Roth, 401k, Keogh, or any other plan in addition to the defined benefit plan. This is all on top of whatever other retirement reserves you set aside.

What if disaster happens? What if you shutter the business? What if you can't come up with the money? Does it put you in hot water? No, you simply close the plan. Notify the IRS, and roll the money into an IRA. What if you decide not to retire? Not a problem; you amend the plan. In other words, these plans are flexible. If you qualify and you can afford to fund it, it usually pays to defer taxes.

SPENDING DOWN RETIREMENT ACCOUNTS

The conventional wisdom is to withdraw money from your taxable accounts first, so that the tax-deferred accounts have the longest time to compound tax-free, and then to withdraw from Roth IRAs last, since they can be left to the next generation where the tax-free payout can be amortized over their lifetime. However, this presupposes that you are likely to spend down most of your assets during your life. If you are going to leave a large estate, a different pecking order may serve you better.

IRA withdrawals are taxed at marginal rates. If you leave a large IRA to your high-earning children, they will pay steep taxes on the withdrawals. On the other hand, if you leave them your taxable investment accounts, they will get a step-up in cost basis, and then your heirs can take the money out either tax-free (as a return of principal) or by paying lower capital gains taxes. In that case, the better tactic is to spend the IRAs down or donate them to charity, letting your kids inherit your taxable accounts and Roth IRAs instead. Note that all these accounts are equally subject to estate tax.

529 PLANS

With 529 plans, we have to distinguish between the ostensible purpose of the plan (helping strapped parents save for college with free after-tax compounding) and other conceivable uses. One other use is to treat the 529 plan as a stealth IRA, albeit one with a 10 percent penalty on withdrawals of earnings. Imagine that you are 30 years old and put $65,000 in a 529 plan, naming yourself as beneficiary. Then, when you are 75, you decide not to go back to school after all and spend the money on riotous living (possibly educational but not covered by the plan).

The better your investment returns and the higher your tax rate, the more quickly this becomes a good deal vs. after-tax savings in taxable accounts. Break evens are typically between ten and twenty years, depending on how the stock market performs in the interim.

Parents who are especially generous and well-heeled could open a 529 plan for their child early on, and then ignore it and pay for their child's college expenses out of pocket, letting the 529 plan continue to compound on the side. The beneficiaries could even be changed to their grandchildren without triggering a taxable event.

HEALTH SAVINGS ACCOUNTS

A Health Savings Account (HSA) is another investment vehicle that is nominally for one purpose but works better as a de facto retirement account. You have to have a high-deductible health care plan (or no plan at all) in order to open an HSA initially. Then, you might contribute $3,100 (single) or $6,250 (family), tax-deductible, with $1,000 catch-up for those 55 and over, often with some type of employer match. The money compounds federal tax-free and tax free in most states (watch out if you live in Alabama, California, New Jersey, New Hampshire, or Tennessee), and can be pulled out tax-free at any time to pay for current medical expenses. These are small sums and many affluent investors will have comprehensive health care coverage that will preclude using Health Savings Accounts. Many who are pre-affluent will have a shot at this, however, and they should take advantage of the opportunity. Note: HSAs are not to be confused with "flex" spending plans that many employers offer, where your unspent money is forfeited at the end of every year.

Leave the account alone and pay for non-covered medical expenses out-of-pocket. Once you are 65, you can draw from your HSA for any purpose without penalty, paying taxes only on money spent for non-medical expenses. A 65-year-old is projected to spend $240,000 on non-reimbursed medical expenses before he or she dies (!)—much of it late in life. This demonstrates the incredible value in setting up an HSA when you are younger and leaving it dormant for decades. Sheryl Rowling, CPA, points out that these accounts are the most powerful retirement savings vehicles because they are triple tax-free: deductible on the front-end, no tax on the earnings, and no tax on withdrawals used for medical expenses.

If your employer offers a matching contribution, they will have pre-selected their own HSA plan administrator. Once you are no longer relying on their largesse, consider transferring your HSA to a plan offering Vanguard funds (such as the one from HSA Administrators), so you don't get eaten alive by high annual fees.

OPENING INVESTMENT ACCOUNTS

When you open an investment account, you quickly have to make a number of decisions with far-reaching implications. Here are a few tips.

- Money Market Funds—You will have a choice between a taxable and a tax-exempt money market fund. Take a moment and compare the after-tax yield on each. Vanguard has a Taxable-equivalent Yield Calculator that will present your best option, and there are numerous similar calculators on the Internet.

- Reinvestment of Dividends and Capital Gains—Automatically reinvest these from your mutual funds if you are pre-retirement. This is a trifling matter but it would spare you a few dollars in reinvesting the proceeds. If you are retired and drawing down the account, you might want to arrange for the dividends and capital gains to be paid out in cash.

■ Beneficiaries—For IRAs, you will want to name specific people as beneficiaries rather than your estate or trust. This will let your heirs pull the money out amortized over their lifetimes instead of being forced to take the money out at an accelerated schedule more pleasing to the IRS.

■ Cost Basis—By default, many investment firms use the obsolete "First In—First Out" tax lot accounting when determining the cost basis for securities that you sell. Change this to "Best Tax," "Tax Optimized," or "Short-term Tax Sensitive," or similar. This will be very useful in deferring taxes. These approaches automatically scan all of your trade lots and earmark the ones with the highest cost basis for sale first, allowing you to realize losses and postpone realizing gains as long as possible.

BUYING AND SELLING

When buying securities in taxable accounts, you do not want to buy a mutual fund that is on the brink of making a taxable distribution—in effect, handing you back the after-tax money you just gave them so it immediately can be taxed again. These distributions usually occur near the end of each quarter, with the biggest distributions issuing in December. You will have to check with the specific fund you are interested in to find out what's forthcoming.

When you go to market to sell, there is no time like the present to track down the cost basis for securities you are liquidating, because you will require this information come April 15th and it may be easier to ascertain while the shares are still in hand.

Unless you are some kind of trader, wait one year before selling appreciated securities so that capital gains receive favorable long-term treatment.

Comb through your holdings periodically for opportunities to harvest tax losses. You may have bought securities in the past that are worth less today than the day you bought them (yes, astonishingly, this can happen). If you sell a security within one year, you can harvest a very desirable short-term capital loss, which you can count against other short-term capital gains or even against ordinary income at tax time. If you held the security more than one year, you can harvest a long-term capital loss, which counts against other long-term capital losses and $3,000 per year may be credited against ordinary income, with carry-overs applied in perpetuity. Not a large sum, perhaps, but every penny counts.

Reviewing your accounts for losses once a year is fine, although if you have an advisor he may do this more frequently. I recently reviewed an account where my software (TRX Total Rebalance Expert) flagged a $5,000 capital loss I could harvest. When I examined the mutual fund in question, I saw a $50,000 capital gain. I called TRX Total Rebalance Expert to notify them of their error, but they turned the tables on me. Within all the individual tax lots that made up this client's holding, most had significant gains, but one lot had a $5,000 loss. Their clever software was telling me to sell just the one individual tax lot registering the loss. This kind of sharpshooting can be very cool if you are willing to go the extra step of identifying individual tax lots when placing sell orders.

The year you retire is a great time to make a final search through your holdings for any unrealized short-term capital losses so that you can debit $3,000 of them against ordinary income while you still have income to report.

Of course, you have to do something with the cash that harvesting generates. Do not buy the fund back within 30 days of having sold it at a loss, or even a substantially identical fund, or it will count as a "wash sale" and the capital gains tax-loss deduction will be disallowed. What funds are substantially identical to each other is open to interpretation. For example, I would not sell one S&P 500 index fund and buy a different S&P 500 index fund and expect to get away with it. But I might sell an S&P 500 index fund and buy a U.S. Total Stock Market index fund. The performance would be similar but there are still meaningful differences in strategy and holdings. Then, 31 days later, I could sell the Total Stock Market index fund and buy back the S&P 500 index fund, if that is what I wanted to do. Never buy as a short-term holding anything that you would not be comfortable keeping as a long-term holding, since a lot can happen in 31 days. You might have to hold it for a year to avoid selling and harvesting a substantial short-term capital gain if there is a sudden jump in the market.

To complicate matters further, some investors harvest capital gains, not losses. If they know capital gains tax rates are going up, and they recognize that they will have to sell the security soon anyway, it can pencil out to pay today for a hamburger Tuesday. Nevertheless, accountants live by the rule that a tax deferred is a tax not paid. If you postpone taxes long enough, your heirs may end up with a tax-free step up in your entire cost basis.

For those who are really motivated, you can sell a mutual fund that is about to make a taxable distribution the day before it goes ex-dividend and switch into a similar (but not substantially identical) fund, provided the sale does not rack up more in capital gains than you avoid through bypassing the distribution. Sometimes this can mean being out of the market for a day, which has its own consequences.

SUCCESS TAX

If you have over $4,100,000 in your tax-deferred accounts such that this will require a minimum distribution of over $150,000 annually when you hit age 70 ½, you will be forced to pay an additional "success tax" of 15 percent on any sum beyond $150,000 that you withdraw. Congratulations on your success! To avoid it, start taking annual withdrawals from these accounts as early as age 59 ½ in order to bring their projected totals below the $4.1 million threshold.

STATE TAXES

Where you live makes a big difference to your tax burden. Table 9.2 (see page 190) shows the taxes faced by a family of three with income of $150,000 a year who live in the largest city in the top ten and bottom ten states for total taxes, including state income tax, property tax, sales tax, and automobile registration taxes.

Analyst Meredith Whitney regularly ranks state finances, and it is interesting to note that five of the states with the top ten highest tax burdens are also the most insolvent by her calculations (Connecticut, New York, Michigan, Ohio, and, it goes without saying, California), whereas only two of the top ten states with the lowest tax burdens (Nevada and Florida) are in poor financial shape. An equal number of the low tax states have finances that are well run (Texas and Washington) by her reckoning, while none of the states with the high tax burdens do. I take this to mean that the high tax states could see their taxes going even higher as they desperately attempt to cover their shortfalls in a tax-and-spend death spiral.

To appraise the utility of moving, say, from Bridgeport to Anchorage, you could plug your financial scenario into *ESPlanner*, and note the change of state residence from CT to AK. Your cost of housing and your property taxes will fall precipitously. If you are seriously contemplating such a move, you will also want to check out Sperling's Best Places "Compare Cities" cost of living calculator to investigate what the cost of goods and services will likely be in the new state.

Table 9.2: Estimated Total State Tax Burdens on $150,000 Income		
Top Ten		
State	Total	%
Connecticut	$23,655	15.8%
New York	$18,077	12.1%
Kentucky	$17,458	11.6%
Philadelphia, PA	$16,302	10.9%
Maine	$16,297	10.9%
Michigan	$16,109	10.7%
Ohio	$15,928	10.6%
California	$15,539	10.4%
Iowa	$15,499	10.3%
Maryland	$15,180	10.1%
Bottom Ten		
State	Total	%
Louisiana	$9,338	6.2%
North Dakota	$7,990	5.3%
Washington	$6,502	4.3%
Texas	$6,310	4.2%
New Hampshire	$6,159	4.1%
Tennessee	$6,092	4.1%
Nevada	$5,836	3.9%
Florida	$5,797	3.9%
South Dakota	$5,647	3.8%
Wyoming	$4,560	3.0%
Alaska	$4,133	2.8%

Don't blithely assume that you can kiss goodbye to your high-tax state and never hear from them again. No, they are looking for a long-term relationship. In California, they suspect you of being a resident if you so much as listened to "Surfer Girl" on the radio. The criteria for California citizenship are a closely-guarded secret. Some of the items believed to be on the list are:

- Did you earn income in California?

- Do you own any property in California?

- How much time do you spend in California?

- Are you a member of a church or synagogue in California?

- Did you have any physicians or dentists in California?

- What about your accountant, lawyer, financial advisor? Are these in California?

- Do you have family in California?

- Your cell number—is it a California area code?

- Do you store any property in California?

- Do you have a boat, car, or plane in California?

- Do you receive mail at any California address?

- Do you give to charities in California?

- When you are in California, do you make any business-related phone calls or send/receive business faxes? Do you contact your office?

■ Are you licensed to practice your profession in California?

■ Do you have any California bank or investment accounts?

About the only way it is hard to be a California resident is if you move in from out-of-state and want to attend Berkeley without paying the substantially higher non-resident tuition. Then the shoe is on the other foot. Now you have to prove that you really are a California resident and not a four-year transient.

Before you start feeling smug because you don't live in California, consider that your high-tax state has a similar checklist. Try to leave New York sometime. Just when you think you're out, they pull you back in.

ESTATE PLANNING

You are going to prepare your estate plan in consultation with your estate attorney, so I will only chime in with a few remarks for your amusement.

As long as you are alive, there is a superego (you) keeping a lid on all the family dynamics. Once you are gone, so is that lid. A lifetime of jealousies and resentments suddenly boils over from the family cauldron and gets focused on the division of your estate. Who did Mommy/Daddy love more? Who didn't get enough and feels she/he is owed? This is a recipe for an ugly scene. It is largely unpreventable, although there are things you can do to make it slightly less contentious.

Treat your children equally. I'm not saying down to the penny. If you get it within a nickel, that may be close enough. In time, with therapy, the others should adjust. When you have coveted personal property to dispose of, make the determinations while you are still alive and inform the children. They will blame you, of course, but if they have to fight over it after you are gone they will only be able to blame each other.

I asked Michele Abernathy and Anne Gifford Ewing of the boutique Los Angeles law firm Gifford, Dearing, and Abernathy for their take on estate planning for the high net worth. I wanted to get the word on the street from people who are in court every day. I went in expecting to be dazzled with talk of CLATs, CLUTs, CRATs, CRUTs, NIMCRUTs, FlipCRUTs, GRATs, QPRTS, IDGTs, SCINs, and QTIPs. Instead, they drilled me on the importance of selecting the right fiduciaries. Why? Because once you have a brilliant estate plan in place (with all the CLATs and CLUTs, etc.), everything is going to depend on the person you select to administer it. The wrong person in this role—someone who is corrupt, self-interested, or otherwise not up to the task—will scuttle your plans, including all of your fancy trusts. They had no shortage of horror stories at their fingertips. The saboteurs can even include ourselves, if we lose mental capacity before we die.

If our spouse or child is not going to be a great choice for trustee, and our pals are all about our age, we are in the unfortunate position of having to shop for an institutional trustee. Ditto if we have sufficient assets that a multi-generational trustee is going to be required. Be wary of ye local bank trust department. There is no incentive for them to do anything except use your money to maximize their own advantage. You can scarcely imagine what a mediocre job most institutional trustees do. Everything is about fees and kickbacks to their favor bank. With two or three percent or more being siphoned off every year, the trust we so painstakingly set up will benefit them more than our heirs. This holds true even if your attorney goes fox hunting with them and can vouch for what clubbable chaps they are. Look very closely at Vanguard's or Fidelity's trust services instead.

Got kids? If your kids are young and you don't have enough ready cash to take them from bobby sox to stockings, an irrevocable life insurance trust (ILIT) is in order. A term life insurance policy goes inside the trust. The money will be free of estate and income taxes and available for bringing up baby. Term insurance may also be needed to pay estate taxes and prevent a forced sale of illiquid assets (your home or business).

Leaving your kids cash can be expensive. Set up a spendthrift trust and give your children the income from it instead. This way, the money that stays inside the trust cannot be attached by creditors or conniving ex-spouses. Missy wants to buy a house? Fine, the trust loans Missy the down payment. Missy wants to set up a business? Fine, the trust becomes a shareholder. Missy gets divorced? Sorry, this money isn't Missy's; it belongs to the trust.

If you really want to ruin your kids' lives, make sure that they receive millions of dollars when they are 21 years old. That way they won't have to work for a living or have any dealings with the real world. Give them a life of indolence and idleness and they will self-destruct in no time.

There is a lot to be said for gifting appreciating assets as early as possible. If you give your kids $13,000 a year in family company stock, this will amount to a much larger gift than if you write them a check for $13,000 cash and then they inherit $10,000,000 in family company stock after it has appreciated over forty years. In that case, they will be forced to give at least half to Uncle Sam (and sell your liquid assets just to pay the taxes).

As already mentioned, 529 Plans are wonderful gifting tools. After three years the money is out of your estate. You and your bride can each make a one-time, five-year $65,000 contribution to as many children and grandchildren as you wish. You also can pay tuition or medical care expenses directly (provided the checks are paid directly to the school or health care provider) without it count-ing against your lifetime gift exemption.

Some assets are more difficult to value for tax purposes than others. A family business vs. an investment account. A house vs. a money market fund. If that valuation is open to interpretation, if there is a discount for illiquidity, this effectively may pass more value to your heirs net of the tax man.

Sixteen states levy estate or inheritance taxes on top of the federal rates, making them more expensive places to shuffle off that mortal coil. New Jersey and Maryland are the worst, levying both estate and inheritance taxes. Many other states have estate taxes that kick in at low exemptions (say, $1 million) before taking their cut (often 16 percent), but this varies. States that will charge you to ferry across that River Styx include Hawaii, Washington (state and DC), Oregon, Minnesota, Illinois, Ohio, Maine, Vermont, New York, Massachusetts, Connecticut, Rhode Island, Delaware, and North Carolina.

My final list of states (New York, Pennsylvania, West Virginia, North Carolina, Tennessee, Colorado, Utah, Idaho, Montana, Wash-ington, Oregon, and California) are states with a Physician Orders for Life-Sustaining Treatment (POLST) program. Signed by patient (or designated surrogate) and doctor, these are for people who ex-pect to die within the year. They provide clear, actionable directives regarding your end-of-life medical care to any health-care providers who may show up. Everyone loves to play doctor and it is surpris-ing how often "do not resuscitate" orders are ignored.

CHARITABLE GIVING

Over your lifetime you will be transforming your human capital into financial capital, and then into social capital. The social capital will either be allocated by the government or by a charity. If you like how the government spends your money, you are all set—do nothing. If you have a different idea, get behind a charity. Money you give to charity is tax deductible today and out of your estate. It is an opportunity to do well by doing good.

Naturally, this isn't as easy as it sounds. Charities are fully aware that they are a captive alternative tax system for the rich, and as you would expect, they provide notoriously poor service at high expense. The only charity I know with a relentless focus on ROI is Mohnish Pabrai's Dakshana Foundation (which is not surprising, since Mohnish runs a hedge fund). There must be others. It is your mission to locate one, so your hard-earned money isn't squandered by self-serving administrators. You need to give with your head as much as with your heart. As a first step, there are community foundations that can provide philanthropic expertise in your region.

While you are doing your due diligence, you need some place to park your charitable dollars, so you can optimize their tax-effectiveness. I love the donor-advised charitable trusts that have been set up by Vanguard, Fidelity, and Schwab for this purpose. They completely obviate the need for family foundations for all but the likes of Bill and Melinda. You donate money to them today, take the tax deduction today, opt for one of their potted asset allocations, and then parcel out the money to charities you elect on any timetable you choose over the rest of your life. Given that Congress will be shaking the high net worth by their heels to get whatever coins they can as our country's finances become threadbare, there is an argument for taking this deduction sooner than later, since the charitable deduction could be eliminated or capped. If you decide to wait, though, you can give your IRA to a charitable trust and let your heirs decide how to make the grants, or leave it with a letter of instruction.

The benefits will make you twist and shout. First, by making the donations while you are still employed and in a high tax bracket, you get the maximum value from the charitable deduction instead of wasting it late in life when you are in a low tax bracket. If you donate highly appreciated stock held more than one year, you sidestep the capital gains tax while getting the current price for your tax deduction. Some people use this type of charitable donation to offset the extra taxes from making a Roth IRA conversion, which can be a nifty maneuver. If you have a lot of appreciated stock from a family business, you can still donate it by putting it into a charitable trust of your own devising.

If you are personally involved with a charity, you may notice that they are more interested in what you are planning to do for them next rather than what you did for them in the past. The past is past. They will treat your ideas with more respect if they hope for more money to come. With a donor-advised trust or a community foundation, unlike with a family foundation, there is no way they can look up how much or how little is still in the piggy bank.

One other idea: if you leave money to a charity in your will, insert a clause that anyone who brings suit against your estate forfeits their right to inherit from it. Charities have been known to aggressively pursue monies they believe were promised to them, even when the donor's circumstances have changed (e.g., the donor has gone to the Land of the Pharaohs and the money has been diverted to other engagements).

Dare I close with a Warren Buffett anecdote? I said to Warren, "You've given so much money to the Gates Foundation, do you ever read about some interesting charity and pick up the phone and say, 'Hey, Bill—this outfit on page A12 in today's *Journal* seems pretty nifty—you might want to give them a look.'"

Warren replied, "I wouldn't dream of doing that. Not in a million years."

Phil: "But you've given him billions of dollars to allocate...."

Warren: "I don't hire a plumber and then stand around telling him what to do. Why would this be any different?"

***

That's all I've got!

I'm going to sign off with a passage from the 1928 *Book of Common Prayer* that specifies the fiduciary duty of the affluent investor:

ALMIGHTY God, whose loving hand hath given us all that we possess; Grant us grace that we may honour thee with our substance, and remembering the account which we must one day give, may be faithful stewards of thy bounty.

Thank you for spending your incredibly valuable time with me. I hope you found something in these pages to help you faithfully steward the bounty with which you have been entrusted.

ACKNOWLEDGEMENTS

No man is an island. Then again, no man is a kumquat. While normally I like to take all the credit, I'd better cough up a few names here since I might need their help in the future.

The tireless exertions of my agent, Bob Diforio, along with Wayne Barr at Barron's Educational Series, led to greenlighting this project, whereupon Editorial Director Kevin Ryan fearlessly slogged his way through the manuscript, coming back alive with many astute suggestions. Finally, when my natural modesty inclined me to hide my book under a bushel, publicist Monique Mallory had me shout it from the rooftops.

You might as well know that I reached out to any number of people smarter than me to tune up the content: Bryan Johnson, Jay Adkisson, Sheryl Rowling, Jim Picerno, Ron Harkey, Bill Dillhoeffer, Michael Phillips, Patrick Burns, Geoff Considine, and Michele Abernathy, to name a few of the better-looking ones. It goes without saying that any errors in the manuscript are all their fault.

Finally, a supersize order of thanks to Ben Stein, to whom this pitiful work is dedicated, and without whom I would be living in a homeless shelter for destitute and aged (over 35) Hollywood writers instead of lounging with my feet up on the desk smoking a Montecristo here at Millionaire Acres.

Phil DeMuth, Ph.D.
Conservative Wealth Management LLC
Los Angeles, California

Index

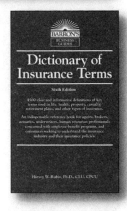
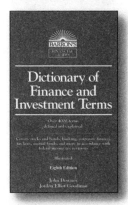